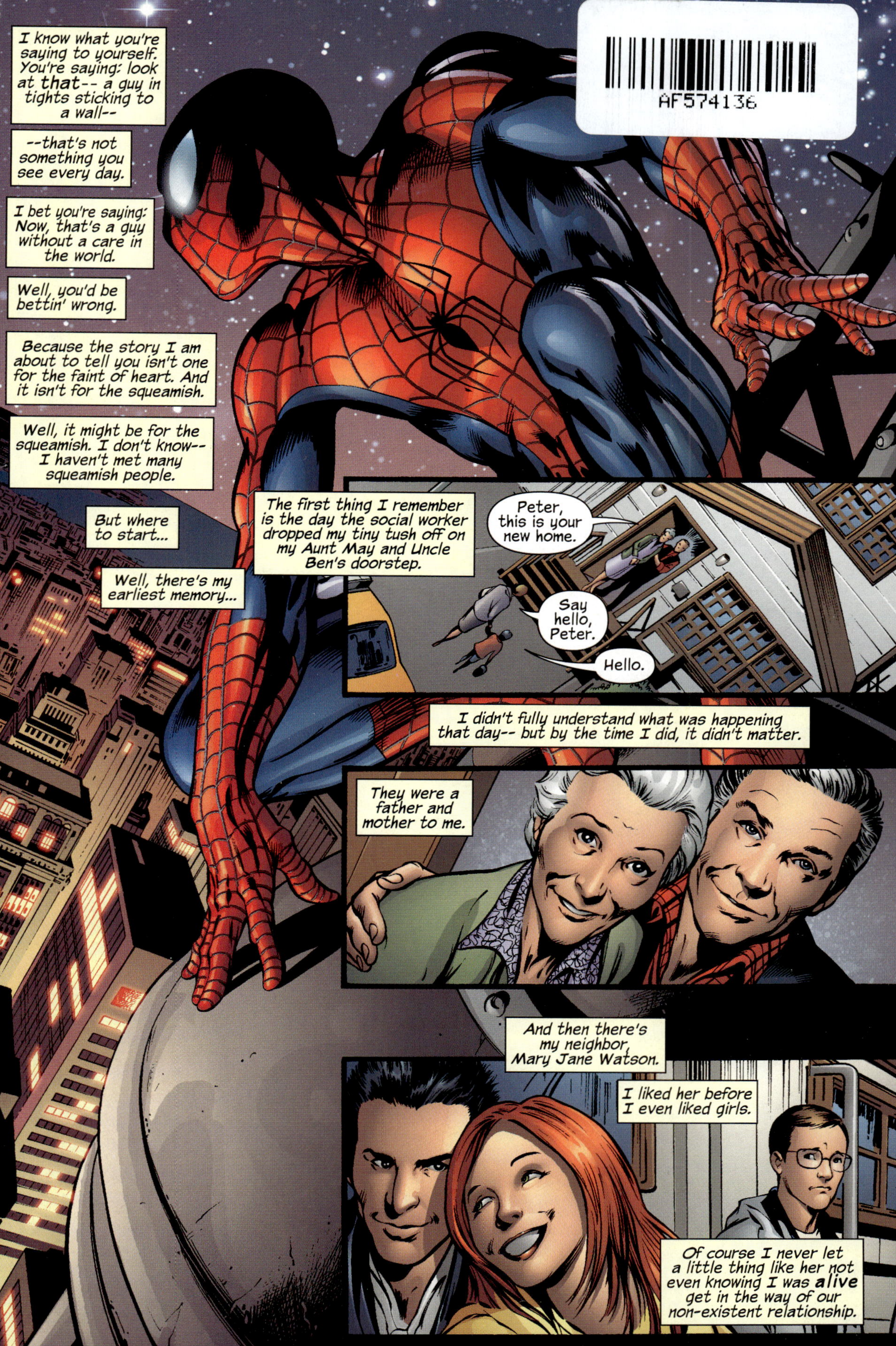

AF574136
I know what you're saying to yourself. You're saying: look at that-- a guy in tights sticking to a wall--
--that's not something you see every day.
I bet you're saying: Now, that's a guy without a care in the world.
Well, you'd be bettin' wrong.
Because the story I am about to tell you isn't one for the faint of heart. And it isn't for the squeamish.
Well, it might be for the squeamish. I don't know-- I haven't met many squeamish people.
But where to start...
Well, there's my earliest memory...
The first thing I remember is the day the social worker dropped my tiny tush off on my Aunt May and Uncle Ben's doorstep.
Peter, this is your new home.
Say hello, Peter.
Hello.
I didn't fully understand what was happening that day-- but by the time I did, it didn't matter.
They were a father and mother to me.
And then there's my neighbor, Mary Jane Watson.
I liked her before I even liked girls.
Of course I never let a little thing like her not even knowing I was alive get in the way of our non-existent relationship.

And then there was the big day to top all big days. The field trip.
A day a science nerd like myself was really looking forward to... an afternoon at the Columbia Genetic Research Institute.
And it started off innocently enough.
With my friend-- my only friend-- Harry Osborn introducing me to his father for the first time.
Peter Parker-- Norman Osborn.
It's an honor to meet you, sir.
Harry tells me you're something of a scientist. I'm something of a scientist myself.

Hey, guys.
MJ.
Hi-- uh--hi. Uh...

Well said, Pete.
Come on.
I'm tellin' ya, that MJ-- WOW! That is-- that is some kind of girl.
And, of course, that was the last thing I wanted to hear. But it's not like I had half a chance with her anyway.

The Columbia Genetic Research Institute...
There are more than 32,000 known species of spiders.
The Genus Salticus can leap up to 40 times its body length.
The Genus Atrax spins a web so strong, it's similar to high-tension bridge building wire.

While the Genus Misumena possesses an uncanny ability to sense danger.
You might even call it a "spider sense."

I'd been looking forward to this demonstration for weeks, but instead I get a demonstration of that jerk Flash Thompson pawing at MJ.
I never knew what she was doing with that guy.

And we have fifteen genetically enhanced spiders for--
Uh-- there's only fourteen.
What?
There's only fourteen in that case.
Hmmm, perhaps one is being observed in the back. Let's move onto the--

--uh--um-- MJ? May I take your picture for the school newspaper.
Oh! Are you serious? Okay. But only if you promise not to make me ugly.

That-- that would be *impossible.*

Aahhh!

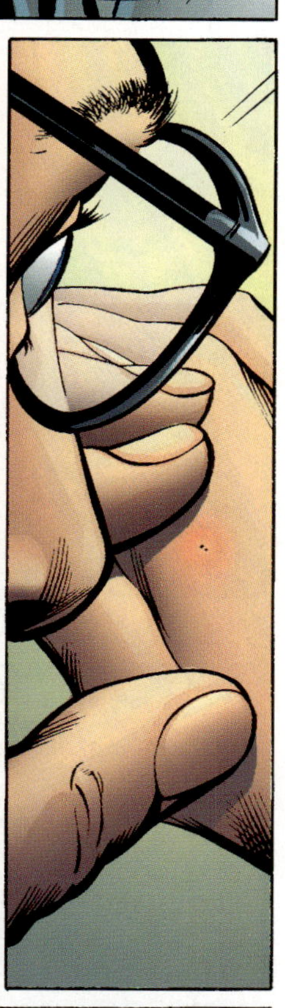

OSCORP.
Osborn, your experiment is taking too long.
You know the military's waiting for your human performance enhancer.
I've already seen your glider. That's not why I'm here.

Gentlemen, the performance enhancer is a complex experiment. The psychological variables alone are--
I'm sorry Osborn, if you don't have concrete results in two weeks, we're pulling the plug and taking the project elsewhere.

The next morning.
Peter, breakfast!
Peter?

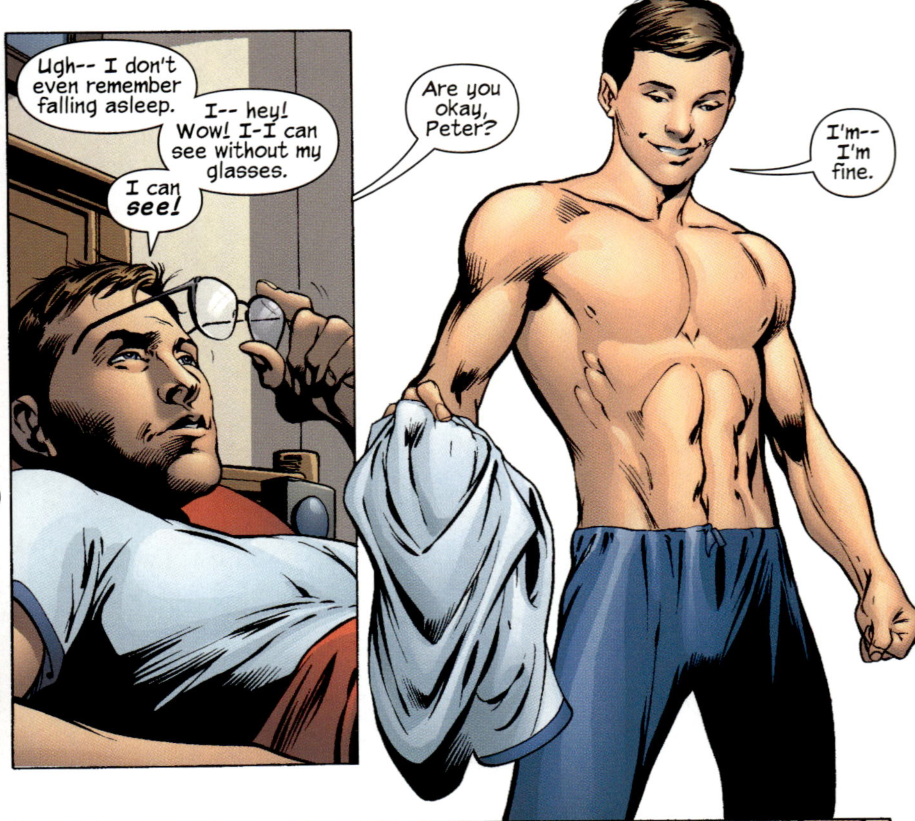
Ugh-- I don't even remember falling asleep.
I-- hey! Wow! I-I can see without my glasses.
I can see!
Are you okay, Peter?
I'm-- I'm fine.

I know I'm going nuts-- even the school cafeteria food tastes great.
I-I've never felt better in my-- uh oh.

I gotta get out of here. I-- oh no!
Aaggh! Parker! You class A spaz!

Was an accident.
My fist breaking your teeth...that's the accident.

All-- all of a sudden I feel funny.
My fingers don't feel right.
This stuff-- it's like string. String coming out of my wrists.

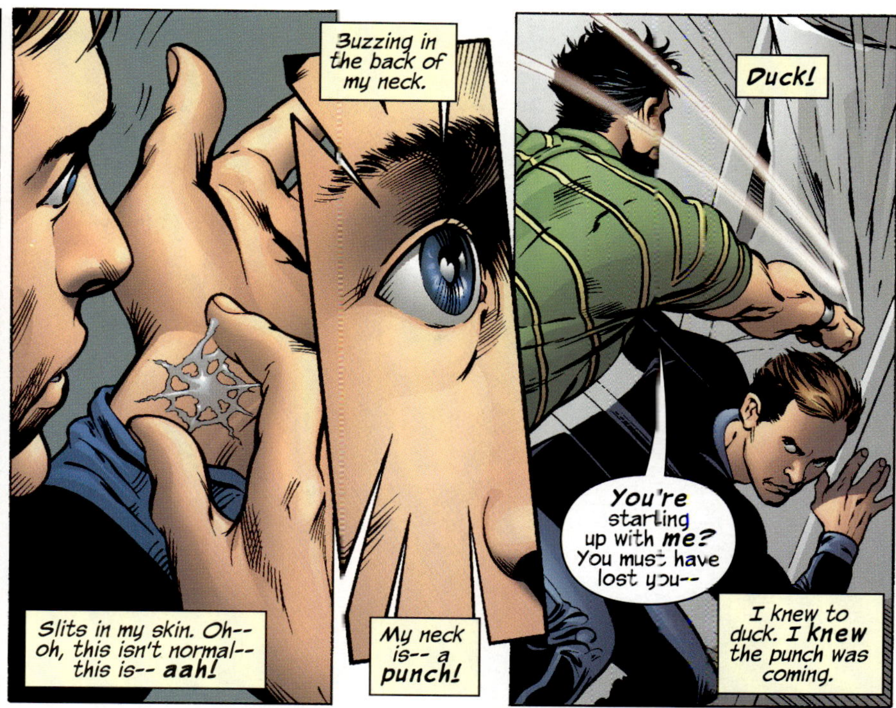
Buzzing in the back of my neck.
Slits in my skin. Oh-- oh, this isn't normal-- this is-- aah!
My neck is-- a punch!
Duck!
You're starting up with me? You must have lost you--
I knew to duck. I knew the punch was coming.

Come here, you little...
Like he's in slow motion--
--I can see the punches before they happen.

Waddaya know! Parker knocked him cold!
No way! Flash just tripped.
Yeah. That hadda be what happened.

Something has happened to me-- something I can't--
The spider.
The spider.
Aaahh hahaha haha!!

Later. The Parker home...

CRASH!

Peter, are you okay?

I'm fine.

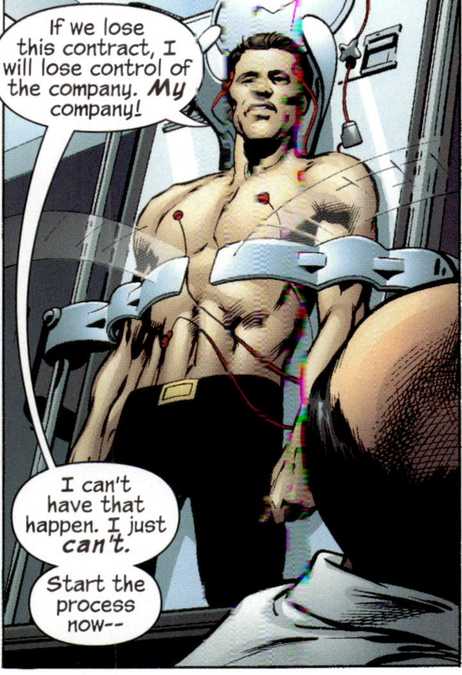

Arghhh!

Mr. Osborn! Wh-what ***happened*** to you?

I have to see Mr. Osborn.
My father isn't well.
It's all right, Harry. She's an employee.

Mr. Osborn, Dr. Stromm is dead.
The lab-- the lab's been destroyed!

The next morning...
Have fun at the library. Wear your seatbelts-- both of you.
Yeah--uh--I'll get something to eat at the library. So don't worry about me for dinner.
I'll be home early for dinner, dear.

Is everything all right with you, Peter?
Yeah, sure.
You know everybody goes through the awkward stages. Everyone does.
Whatever you've been going through lately-- I've been there, too.
I doubt it.

Just like your father. You're so smart, smarter than I'll ever be.
The world is out there just waiting to see what you're going to bring to it. And that's power, Peter. Power.
Okay.
And with great power there must also come great responsibiity.
Okay!

I know I'm not your father.
Then stop pretending to be. Just let me have a moment to think.
Okay, Peter. Fine.

Tsk-- I shouldn't have snapped at Uncle Ben like that, he doesn't know how crazy my life is.

Well, maybe after I use these powers of mine to start helping to pay the bills, I'll just come clean.
Okay, time to see what these powers are worth.

--And Bone Saw McGraw wins again!
Ain't no one can beat me-- no one!
I'm the greatest there is!
C'mon, ya bunch'a spineless weaklings!
Who else wants'a be crushed by Bone Saw?
I'd like to try.
Your insurance paid up?
Let me worry about that.
It's your funeral.
Ladieees and gentlemen! We have a new vict--eh, a new contender!
He calls himself Spider-Man!
Let's hope there's a doctor in the house!
Well, that's encouraging.
How d'ya want it, Shorty? A broken leg or a busted back?
Oh man, I'm not good with multiple choice.

Whoah, it's called deodorant big guy.
I don't expect you to know how to *spell* it--
--but if you going to be those big hairy around, it's the you could
The guy in the spider suit beat Bone Saw!
Yay, Spider-Man!
Spider-Man!
It was like beating
The ad said the winner gets $3,000-- not fifty.
The ad said nothin' about kids. Kids get *fifty bucks.*
I really need that money.
I missed the part where that's my problem. You come back next week and we'll see what we can do --
Yeah, *that'll* happen.

Stop that man!

Grab him!
Hold him!
He snatched cash from the till!
Don't let him reach the elevator!

What's with you?
What?
All-- all you had to do was hold him, trip him-- *anything.*
I missed the part where that's my problem.
But--you just *stood* there and let him get away.

Well, that was a big bust.
Better get back to the library and meet Uncle Ben. I should just sit down and tell him what's happening with--
--Aahh, that buzzing is happening again.

Stay back, fella. This is a crime scene.
I'm sorry, son. There's nothing you--
POLICE
NO!!! Uncle Ben!!

It was just a random car-jacking. We got the call-- they're on the guy.
He's heading South, down 5th Avenue. They'll get him. Don't you worry, they'll get him.

No!
He's *mine!*
This ride's ending *NOW!*
Guh-- huh huh h-- what was that?

Cops all around the place!
I'll have'ta shoot my way out!
It's not the cops you've got to worry about.
You ruined my life!! You killed an innocent--
--oh no...
You're the guy from the wrestling arena.
I just stood there--and let you go.
And now--because of that--Uncle Ben is dead!

All right! Okay, I don't know what's going on here, freak!

But you're buying my way **out** of this!

You little-- hey-- back up--

--get away or I'll--

AAGGUH!

He's gone!

How? No one came out the door!

Quest Aerospace.
One week later.
Well, you people at Quest finished your armor prototype faster and more efficiently than Osborn could.
So, I am going to recommend to the Pentagon that the full contract be awarded to you immediately.
Your country needs you.
QUEST
Uh-- Tower?
There's something coming right at me! I can't read it on my-- it's coming right--
What was that? Was that part of the test?
Oh my god! What is that thing?
It-- it looks like a demon!
OSCORP
OsCorp extends its deepest sympathies to the friends and families of our peers at Quest Aerospace
But I promise that we at OsCorp will do our best to hold to the high standards to which our friendly competition brought us.

Come on, Peter, you and me in the big city. I'm getting this huge loft.
There's tons of room for you.
I don't know--I like to pay my own way.
My dad is already paying for it. You'll buy books instead--
Well, let me think about it.

Your aunt seems to be having the time of her life.
Well, she sacrificed enough to get me here--she deserves a little fun.
She's hitting it off with my dad--that's entirely weird.
Mr. Osborn, Peter has told me so much about you.
Your nephew is a remarkable boy.

He made the Honor Roll!
As well he should.
Dad, I asked Peter to move in next semester--I think he needs a little arm-twisting though.
Peter, we need you to keep Harry out of trouble. Maybe a little of your good attitude will rub off on him.

I'll think about it. It's a tempting offer.

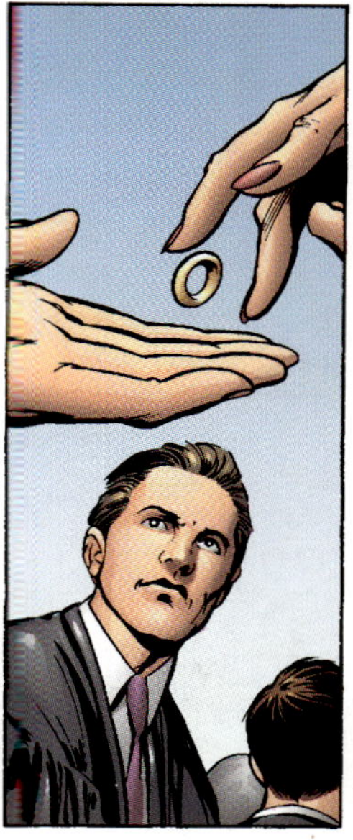

Eh, yes, Mr. Osborn, I'll try to be a good influence on Harry.

I can't make a play for MJ when my best friend is also after her.
Anyway, why kid myself? How could I ever compete with a millionaire's son?
But I've got to stop thinking about myself and consider the bigger picture.
I can't get Uncle Ben's last words to me out of my mind.
"With great power there must also come great responsibility."
I've got to use my new powers-- to do good--
--as Uncle Ben would have wanted.
This is the last store *you'll* ever rob!
Don't worry, lady. This creep's mugging days are over!
He may be outside the law--
--but I like his style.
BANK
COURTESY OF YOUR FRIENDLY NEIGHBORHOOD SPIDER-MAN
Don't tell *me* Spider-Man's human.
I seen it buildin' a nest on top of a roof.
Wait'll his wife learns he's runnin' around at night in tights!
With all those webs, he ought to be cited for littering.
One thing's for sure-- our hero gives the city something to talk about.
Hey, this could be easy money for me! And the career break I've been looking for.
OR CASH
PHOTOS
OF
SPIDER-MAN!

It's not hard to take action photos of yourself--
--when you've hung a pre-focused, automatic camera on webbing nearby!
The office of J. Jonah Jameson, publisher of the Daily Bugle.
Crap! Crap! Crap! Did you actually look through the camera when you took these?
Out of focus - crap
Oh-- Hmmm...
I'll give you fifty for the bunch.
That seems kind of low. Actually, I was hoping for a job.
A job? What do you think this is?
A place that hires people?
Well, this isn't a halfway house for wayward amateur photographers, this is a great metropolitan newspaper.
But I need--
You need a job like I need a new haircut-- just be a man and make a name for--
DAILY BUGLE 50¢
NY CHEERS NEW HERO
We got the headline layout: New York Cheers New Hero.
Cheers?! Cheers?! I don't hear cheers. I hear fear.

Fear sells newspapers.
DAILY BUGLE
NEW YORK'S FINEST DAILY NEWSPAPER
FEARS COSTUMED COWARD
Shouldn't we let the public decide what--

I--uh--think he's right. The word on the street--
What is this kid still doing here? Recess is over, go back to class.
As for this Spider-Man--that costume *reeks* of cowardice.
He's up to some shenanigans or he wouldn't wear a mask.
He'd be in here right now giving me the interview of the *year* instead of skulking around in the shadows.

I still don't see why you have to *bad mouth* him when all he did was--
All right. All right-- if you're going to loiter, loiter around the *World Unity Festival*.
Get something I can print and I'll give you some lunch money.

OsCorp industries board meeting.
We have something to tell you, Norman.
Fine. I'm listening.
That's why we have these meetings.
To give my directors a chance to air their views.
Profits are up, costs are down. Business has never been better.

That's why we've decided to sell the company!

But--you can't!
It's my company. I built it.

That's true, Norman. But we have the votes.
We'll announce the sale right after the World Unity Festival.

The World Unity Festival in New York's Times Square.
Might as well snap some pix before the dull speeches start.
Oh, there's Harry with Mary Jane
Just my luck. She ditches Flash and then my best friend takes over.
Huh? Maybe I have a-- oh no!
That buzzing in the back of my head again.

Wow! I heard there'd be entertainment!
But I never expected anything like this!
Who is he? How does he fly that thing?
Is that our glider?
Did you arrange this?
Of course not!

I'm falling!
Mary Jane!
Where'd she go?
Can't see her through the smoke!
Harry-- help me!
Hang on! Don't let go!
I'll find a way-- to reach you!
Well, well! If it isn't the sniveling board of OsCorp!
Let's see what good all your votes will do you now!
It's no use! You're too far away!
Stay there! I'll try to get a rope!

Aaaww, you got your theme day all wrong.
Green Crazy Lunatic costume day was last Friday.
That tent broke his fall!
The glider's zooming down to him!

That globe replica! Knocked off its base!
It'll crush anyone below!
Momma!
Billy!
Gotcha!
I surrender!
Should'a shot me while you had the chance!
This is crazy. What is that thing?

Wave goodbye for the cameras!
That armor of his almost broke my knuckles!
So the time has come to take my leave.
That glider-- obeys his every command!
But before I depart this vale of tears--
Here's a taste of my glider's weaponry!
Sheesh! With that flying gizmo, he's like a one-man army!
Bored so soon with our little game, my spidery friend?
You won't escape me so easily.
He'll haveta wait.
Mary Jane needs me!

She's still clinging to that wall.
And Harry can't reach her.
I shouldn't have delayed so long!
Hang on, MJ -- I'm coming!
I wouldn't bet on that!
You and I are going for a little ride.
Because I want to show you--
--what happens to those who interfere with me!!
If that's your idea of fun--
--then you'll get a big laugh out of this!
Big mistake, Spider-Man.

At least he knocked me near to where MJ is!
Please-- can you get me off here--
--before this slab breaks loose?!!
I'll answer for him, if I may!
His answer's "no," because--
My eyes! What--??!
For a guy whose mouth doesn't move, you sure do like to hear your-self talk.
And this'll make your glider harder to handle!
The slab's tilting! I-I'm sliding off!
NOOOO!

I can't lose you now!
What have you done?!
Now you'll be killed too!
Not if my webbing holds out!
It held!
I--I don't know how to thank you.
Do you have any cash on you?
What?
Just kidding.
Who--who are you?
Your friendly neighborhood Spider-Man.
And that's copyrighted and trademarked so don't even think of stealing it!

Norman Osborn's penthouse.
The next day.
TIMES SCARE
SPIDER-MAN GREEN GOBLIN TERRORIZE CITY
BUGLE
YORK'S FINEST DAILY NEWSPAPER
FINAL
Partly cloudy, chance of snow. High 25-30. Details p.2

How could that have happened? And-- where was I?

My board members, all killed!
No! it's-- it's impossible!
OsCorp Board Mem Kill

Why can't I remember?
Because you don't want to remember.

Who said that? Who's there?
Follow the cold shiver running down your spine.

That voice-- it's like mine.
But where's it coming from?

Wake up, Osborn. You're me. You're the Green Goblin.
We killed the directors-- just like you wanted.
Now there's only one man who can stop us.
Unless we make him our ally.

Who? Who is it?

You're looking at him!

The Green Goblin! Made it up myself! All these guys need a name!
Who says the internet is killing print media--we've got the Green Goblin.
Ms. Brant!! Get the copyright office on the phone. I want a quarter every time someone says the words Green Goblin.
These costumed freaks make my skin crawl, but they sure move papers.
You can go now, kid. If I need you, I'll call you.
DAILY BUGLE
Someone call the police!
Someone get a camera!
I'm looking for Spider-Man!
Who's the photographer who took his pictures?
Talk, if you value your worthless life!
I--I don't know what you're talking about!
So, I'm curious, what are the rustoleum bills on an outfit like that?
Spider-Man!

This time I'm ready for you.
Have a whiff of sleeping gas.
Sweet dreams, web-head!
That was just to show you who's top gun around here!
C'mon, wake up. I'm a busy little goblin.
This is your lucky day, bug-eyes.
I'm offerin' you the chance to team up with me.
Between the two of us, we can turn this town upside down!
I don't know.
Upside down might make me dizzy.
I'm gonna take that as a "maybe."
So think about it, hear?
'Cause if you don't come aboard--
--I'll crush you like the insect you are!

The next day...

Hey, lady, don'tcha know it ain't safe t'walk around here alone at night?
Yeah, y'might run inta some bad guys who'll try t'rob ya!
Lucky for you ya met us instead.

We'll take everythin' from ya so the bad guys won't get it!
In a pig's eye you will, you creeps!

Hey, the chick's a real scrapper.
We like that.
C'mon, let's git it over with!

So you're in a rush, are you?

Maybe I can help speed things along.

Oops! 'Scuse me.
Sometimes my enthusiasm carries me away.

Aww, did I drop you?
Just call me butter-fingers!

Spider-Man!
This is the second time you've saved me.
Looks like it's becoming a habit.

I still don't know who you really are, or where you're from.
Or how you do what you do-- or why you do it.
I'm from a galaxy far, far away?
What?
Kidding.

Thank you--

--Spider-Man.

A fire-- in that deserted building!
There's someone trapped in the flames!
I'm coming! Hold on-- hold on!!
Don't be afraid...
...just yell so I can...
Wow, you fell for that pretty good, webs.
You-- you started this fire? *Why?*
You're insane!
Innocent people could die from this.
A little attention grabber just for you.
I need an answer! In or out?

A life lesson, kid, and this one is on the house...
No one is innocent!
Aagghh!!
Don't! You'll bring down that fiery beam!
So it's safe to say you're a "the glass is half empty" kind of gal.
I knew it! You're afraid to stay and fight!
But running away won't save you!
We'll meet again! A goblin never forgets!
Blood! I wounded him!
You had your chance, Spider-Man.
Now, it's only a matter of time...

Thanksgiving dinner at Harry and Peter's college apatment.
Harry, this is a wonderful idea of your and Peter's.
My pleasure, Aunt May.

In times like these, with so much crime and violence...
I'm so glad my son Harry has such good and decent friends.
I can't imagine what can be keeping Peter.
I think I hear someone coming now.

Hi, everybody. Sorry I'm late.

Peter-- is that blood on your sleeve?

It's nothing. Just a scratch.

Excuse me, I've got to leave.
Something has come to my attention.
Dad, what are you doing?
Sorry. You entertain your guests, son.

Dad, wait! I planned this whole thing so you could meet Mary Jane.

I'm in love with her. I want to ask her to mar--

Not a chance! Forget her. She's only after your money, do you understand?

How can you say that? You hardly know her.

She's trailer trash from Queens, Harry.

Trade up before she squeezes you dry.

Why are you putting on your coat? Where are you going?

I think it best that I leave.

I've learned who Spider-Man is.
He's Peter Parker.

Now you must tell me what to do.
Wake up and smell the roses, Osborn.
You are me!

Now get this through your thick skull--
--why fight the powerful Spider-Man when you can attack the nerdy Peter Parker?
And get 'im where he's most vulnerable--through someone he loves.

My dearest, darling, Ben. Will I ever stop missing you?
And poor, dear Peter--

He'll no longer be able to look to you for guidance.
I just pray we'll be together again some time, somewhere--somehow.

You may be joining him sooner than you think!

Welcome--to your worst nightmare.

EMER
Aunt May!
She's had a bad shock, son.
But I think she'll pull through.
That injection will help you to rest, Mrs. Parker.
Those horrible yellow eyes, that grotesque, demonic face...
Yellow eyes! Demonic face! It had to be-- the Goblin!
He attacked Aunt May to get at me!
It means-- he knows who I am!
Peter-- listen, dear.
If anything happens to me-- you'll be-- all alone
I want you-- to call Mary Jane. She-- cares about you.
Why do you say that?
A woman-- can sense such things.
Look, Aunt May, don't you worry about me, or Mary Jane or anything at all.
As for the Green Goblin, I promise you this--
He will never bother you again!
You stay away-- from that evil man, dear.
Now go. Call Mary Jane. For me.
I'll do it to make Aunt May happy.
There's no way she can know how MJ feels about me.
I've been waiting for your call, Parker. Can Spider-Man come out to play?
Wait a minute! This isn't Mary Jane's voice on the phone!
If you want to see the girl alive, come to the Queensboro Bridge.
You have ten minutes!

There's the bridge, but where--?
Wait a minute! That cable car--
Why is it shaking that way?
You're just in time, Spider-Man.
I'm about to offer you a choice.
You can either save the girl, or the people on that tram.
Because I'm tired of holding them both!
He's about to push MJ to her death.
But if he drops that cable, everyone in the tram will fall, too!
NOOO!
Happy landings, all!
I can catch MJ!
But--the tram!

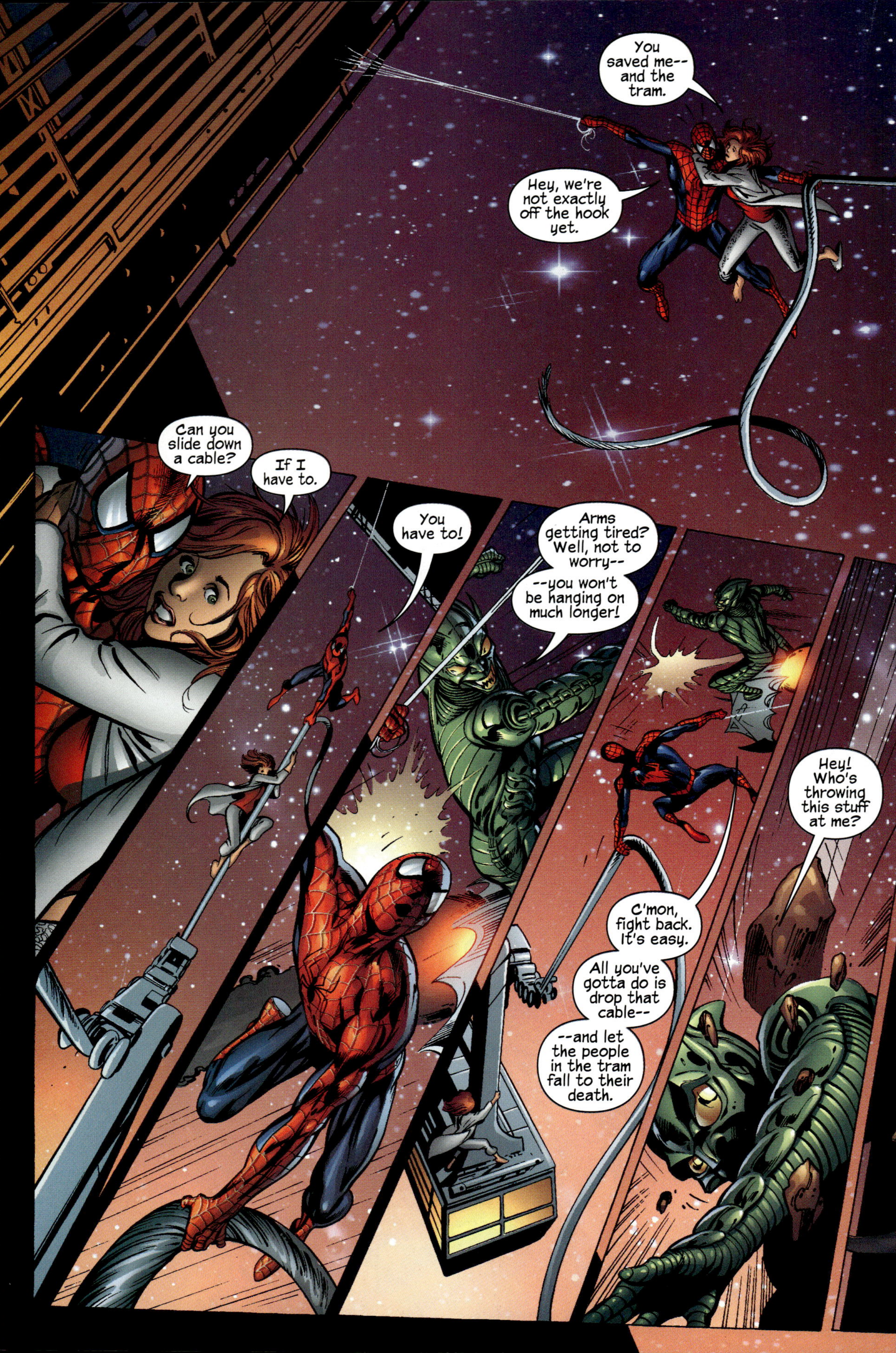
You saved me--and the tram.
Hey, we're not exactly off the hook yet.
Can you slide down a cable?
If I have to.
You have to!
Arms getting tired? Well, not to worry--
--you won't be hanging on much longer!
C'mon, fight back. It's easy.
All you've gotta do is drop that cable--
--and let the people in the tram fall to their death.
Hey! Who's throwing this stuff at me?

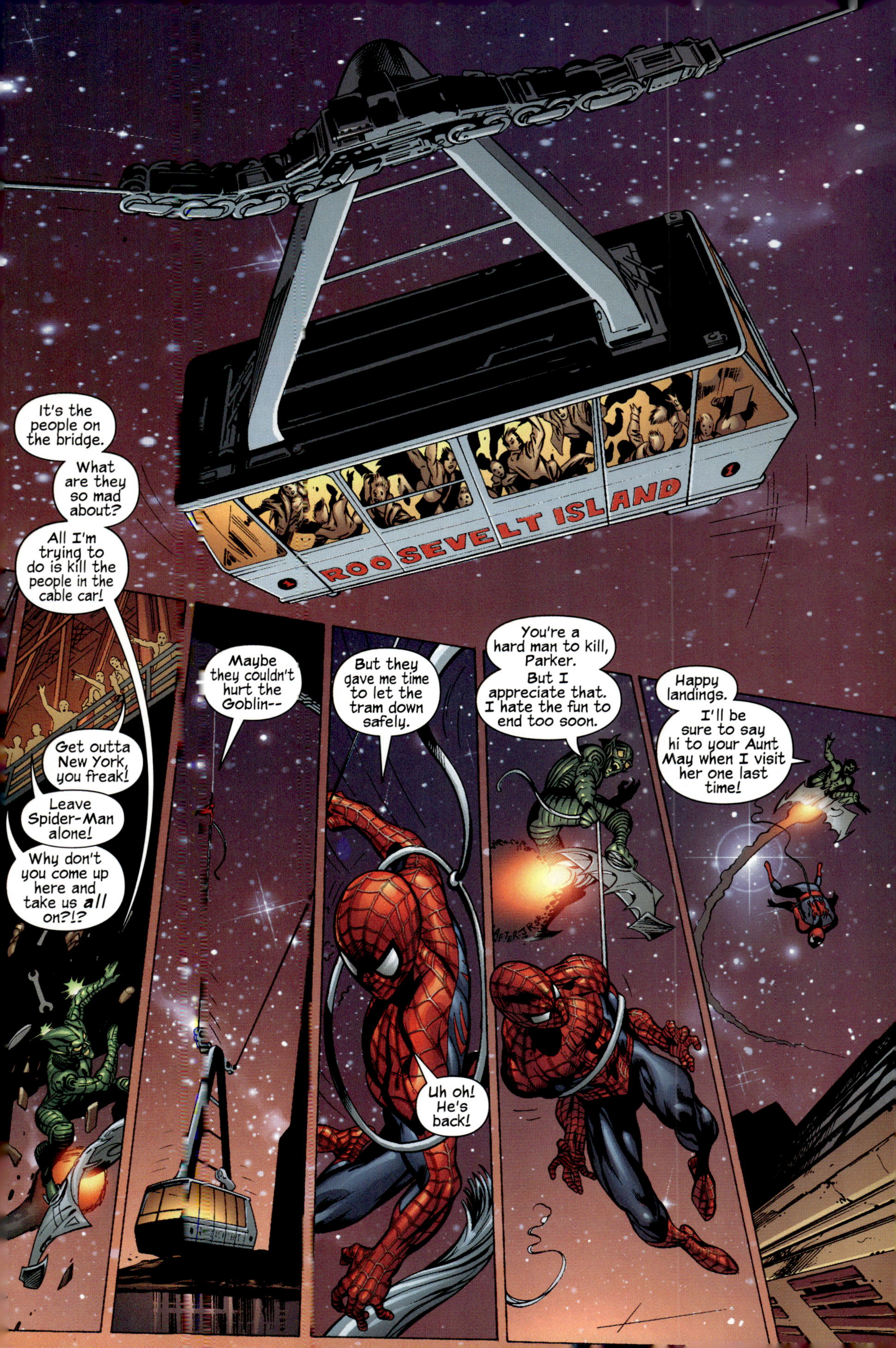
ROOSEVELT ISLAND
It's the people on the bridge.
What are they so mad about?
All I'm trying to do is kill the people in the cable car!
Get outta New York, you freak!
Leave Spider-Man alone!
Why don't you come up here and take us all on?!?
Maybe they couldn't hurt the Goblin--
But they gave me time to let the tram down safely.
Uh oh! He's back!
You're a hard man to kill, Parker.
But I appreciate that. I hate the fun to end too soon.
Happy landings.
I'll be sure to say hi to your Aunt May when I visit her one last time!

You shouldn't have mentioned Aunt May like that Goblin.
You shouldn't have opened your mouth!!
Aaagghh!!
Ready, little man?
This is the wrap-up!
Get up, you **murderer!!** Get up and finish what you--
No, Peter-- it's not me you want.
It's him, the Goblin. He's the bad one.

Don't you understand? I'm your friend.
I'd never do anything to hurt you.
It was the Goblin. It was always the Goblin.
I tried to stop him, but he's too strong.
I only want to help you-- you and your dear Aunt May.
KLIK

No one needs to know Norman Osborn's terrible secret.
It would break poor Harry's heart.
Dad!
What happened? Is he-- dead?
You killed him! You killed my father!
You'll pay for this Spider-Man.
You won't be able to hide from me forever.
He was the only real family I had, Peter.
And Spider-Man murdered him.
But you Peter, you've always been there for me. You're a great friend.
And one day? One day he's going to pay for what he did or me.

Hey, Peter...
Hi MJ-- you doing okay?
I guess. But listen, I've wanted to talk to you alone.
When I was about to die-- when I was hanging off that bridge and I thought I was going to die...

BEN PARKER
...there was only one face that popped into my mind. One face.

Robbie, for the last time-- don't call that weasly wall-crawler a hero in our headlines!
Get real, JJ! What else would you call someone who saved everybody on that tram?
I'd call him lucky! You know I hate vigilantes!
Well, most of our readers love this one!
What are Parker's clothes doing in the office?
Why can't I be surrounded with yes-men like other bosses?
So what if superheroing is tougher than I thought?
So what if some people think I'm one of the bad guys?
So what if my life'll always be in danger?
This is my blessing. This is my curse.
I'm Spider-Man.
THE END!

Experience firsthand the formidable shadow everybody's favorite wall-crawler casts over his not-so-friendly neighborhood as the hottest creators in comics spin stories of ordinary people caught in ...

SPIDER-MAN's TANGLED WEB

BWA-HA-HA-HA.
ONE QUICK CHARGE INCAPACITATED THE POLICE.

NO ONE CAN STOP ME NOW!
NOT SO FAST, ELECTROCUTIONER! WHY NOT TRY YOUR LUCK AGAINST THE CHARISMATIC, NEIGHBORLY...

INSECT MAN

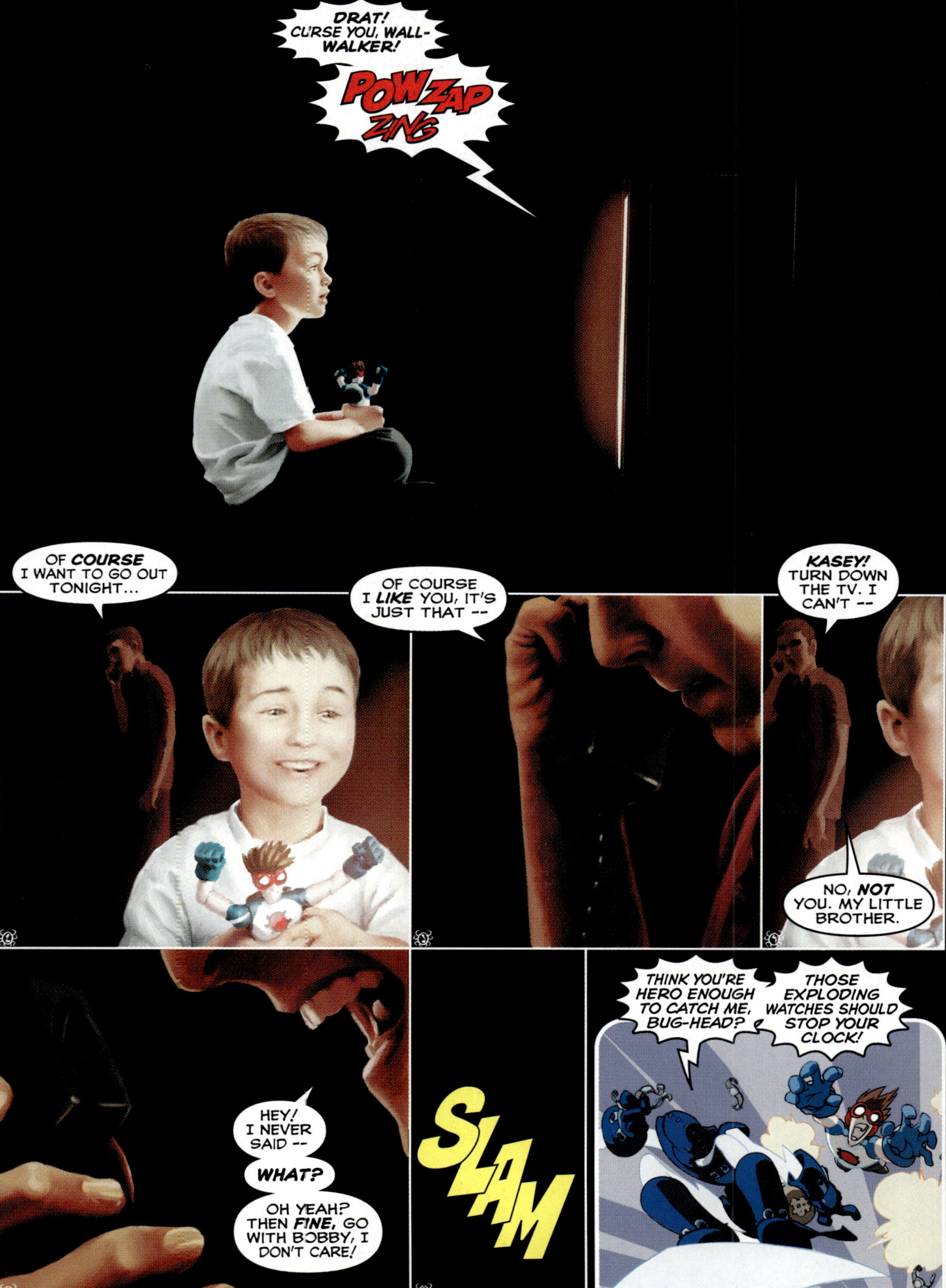
DRAT! CURSE YOU, WALL-WALKER!
POW ZAP ZING
OF COURSE I WANT TO GO OUT TONIGHT...
OF COURSE I LIKE YOU, IT'S JUST THAT --
KASEY! TURN DOWN THE TV. I CAN'T --
NO, NOT YOU. MY LITTLE BROTHER.
HEY! I NEVER SAID --
WHAT?
OH YEAH? THEN FINE, GO WITH BOBBY, I DON'T CARE!
SLAM
THINK YOU'RE HERO ENOUGH TO CATCH ME, BUG-HEAD?
THOSE EXPLODING WATCHES SHOULD STOP YOUR CLOCK!

WHO NEEDS STUPID GIRLS, ANYWAY?
BOYS... ≯COUGH≮ SETTLE DOWN! DON'T MAKE ME GET OUTTA BED! ≯COUGH≮
OH GREAT. SHE OUTTA MEDS AGAIN?
MOM'S BEEN CRYING.
A LOT.
YEAH. I KNOW.
STOP FILLING YOUR BRAIN WITH THAT WORTHLESS JUNK, KASEY.
IT'S NOT JUNK.
Uh-Oh. IF HE REACHES THAT LIGHTNING ROD ON TOP OF THE STATE BUILDING IT COULD BE LIGHTS OUT!

KA-KRACK-A-BOOM!!!

INSECT-BOY, YOU'VE BEEN CHARGED WITH THREE COUNTS OF FAILING TO RECOGNIZE MY GREATNESS, FOUR ACTS OF ATTEMPTED POWER OUTAGES...

WHY DO YOU **KEEP** THESE STUPID COMIC BOOKS? WHY DO YOU EVEN **WANT** THEM?

BECAUSE **DAD** GAVE THEM TO ME.

YOU DON'T EVEN **REMEMBER** DAD. YOU WERE TOO YOUNG WHEN HE **SPLIT**.

JUST BECAUSE DAD DIDN'T LEAVE **YOU** ANYTHING --

I DON'T **WANT** ANYTHING FROM THAT **LOSER**.

ESPECIALLY NOT SOME STUPID **SUPER-HERO** CRAP.

SUPER HEROES ARE LAME.

...AND OVER A DOZEN **INFURIATING ONE-LINERS!** INSECT-BOY, YOU'VE --

CLICK

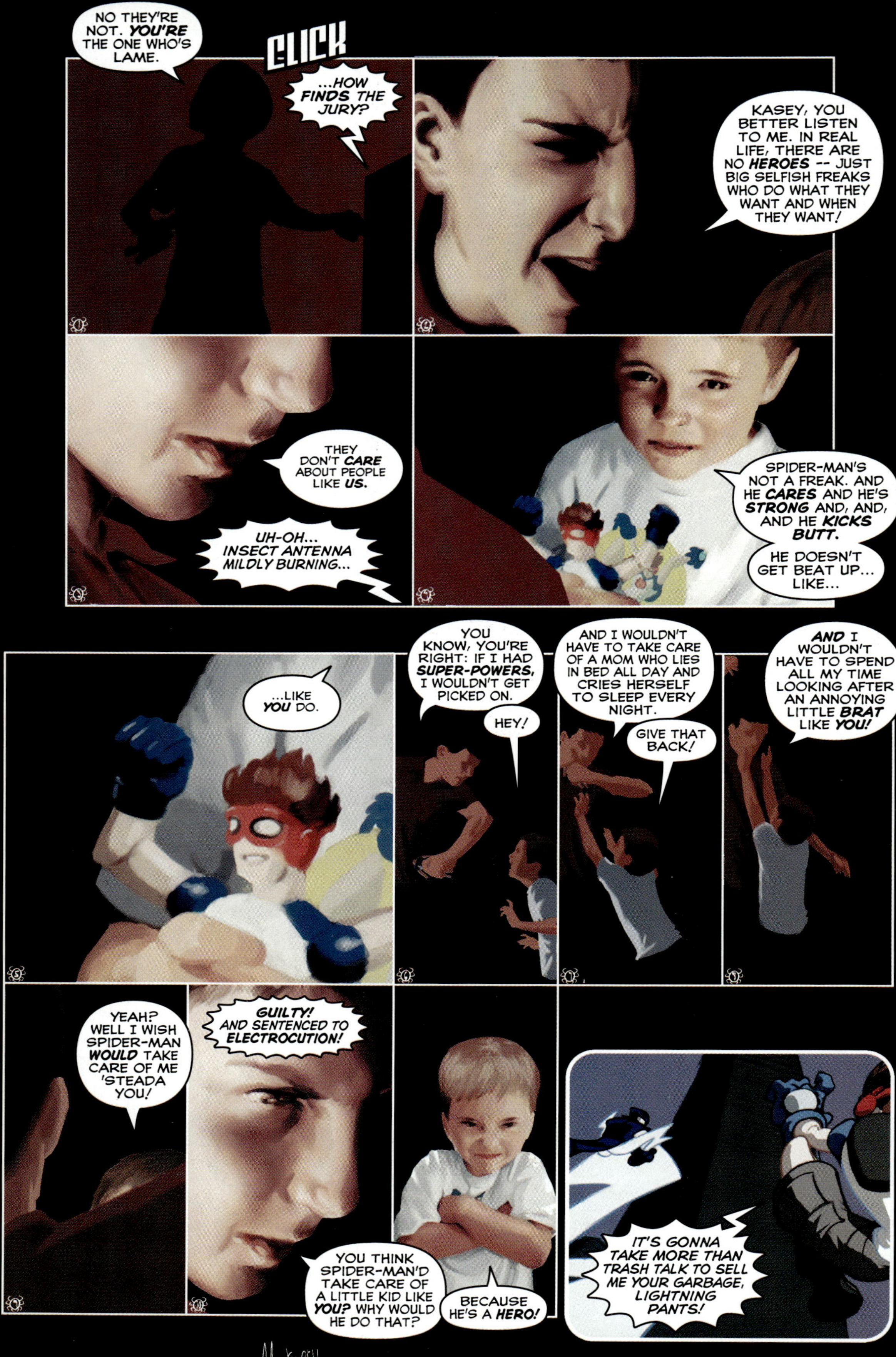

NO THEY'RE NOT. ***YOU'RE*** THE ONE WHO'S LAME.

CLICK

...HOW ***FINDS*** THE JURY?

KASEY, YOU BETTER LISTEN TO ME. IN REAL LIFE, THERE ARE NO ***HEROES*** -- JUST BIG SELFISH FREAKS WHO DO WHAT THEY WANT AND WHEN THEY WANT!

THEY DON'T ***CARE*** ABOUT PEOPLE LIKE ***US.***

UH-OH... INSECT ANTENNA MILDLY BURNING...

SPIDER-MAN'S NOT A FREAK. AND HE ***CARES*** AND HE'S ***STRONG*** AND, AND, AND HE ***KICKS BUTT.***

HE DOESN'T GET BEAT UP... LIKE...

...LIKE ***YOU*** DO.

YOU KNOW, YOU'RE RIGHT: IF I HAD ***SUPER-POWERS,*** I WOULDN'T GET PICKED ON.

HEY!

AND I WOULDN'T HAVE TO TAKE CARE OF A MOM WHO LIES IN BED ALL DAY AND CRIES HERSELF TO SLEEP EVERY NIGHT.

GIVE THAT BACK!

AND I WOULDN'T HAVE TO SPEND ALL MY TIME LOOKING AFTER AN ANNOYING LITTLE ***BRAT*** LIKE ***YOU!***

YEAH? WELL I WISH SPIDER-MAN ***WOULD*** TAKE CARE OF ME 'STEADA YOU!

GUILTY!* AND SENTENCED TO *ELECTROCUTION!

YOU THINK SPIDER-MAN'D TAKE CARE OF A LITTLE KID LIKE ***YOU?*** WHY WOULD HE DO THAT?

BECAUSE HE'S A ***HERO!***

HERO!? WHEN YOU GROW UP LIKE ME YOU'RE GOING TO FIND OUT THERE ARE NO *HEROES*.
STOP IT!
THE ONLY PERSON YOU CAN DEPEND ON IS *YOURSELF*.
STOP IT!
IT DOESN'T MATTER HOW *COOL* YOU THINK THAT FREAK IS --
-- BECAUSE HE DOESN'T CARE ABOUT *ME* --
STOP IT!
-- OR *YOU* --
STOP IT!
-- AND YOU ARE NEVER, *EVER*, GOING TO MEET HI--
CRASH
LET'S FIND OUT!

SPIDER-MAN...?

KASEY, WATCH OUT! HE COULD BE...
SPIDER-MAN!
...Uhhh
KASEY, LISTEN TO ME! I'M NOT GOING TO LET YOU GET HURT.
JUST CALM DOWN AND WE'LL CALL THE POLICE.
NOT SUCH A GOOD IDEA, SPORT.
TAKE A WALK, KIDS. GO WATCH TV OR SOMETHING.
KASEY, LET'S GO.

I'VE GOT BUSINESS WITH THE BUG.

I HOPE YOU'VE GOT YOUR EYES CLOSED UNDER THAT MASK, SPIDER-MAN...
DON'T LOOK, KASEY!
WE HAVE TO HELP!
THIS ISN'T A CARTOON, KASEY! JUST STAY DOWN AND --
BUT HE'S GONNA KILL HIM!
HEY, THAT'S WHAT SUPER-VILLAINS DO. NOW JUST STAY --
KASEY!
...'CAUSE HERE COMES THE BIG WHITE LIGHT.
BOINK

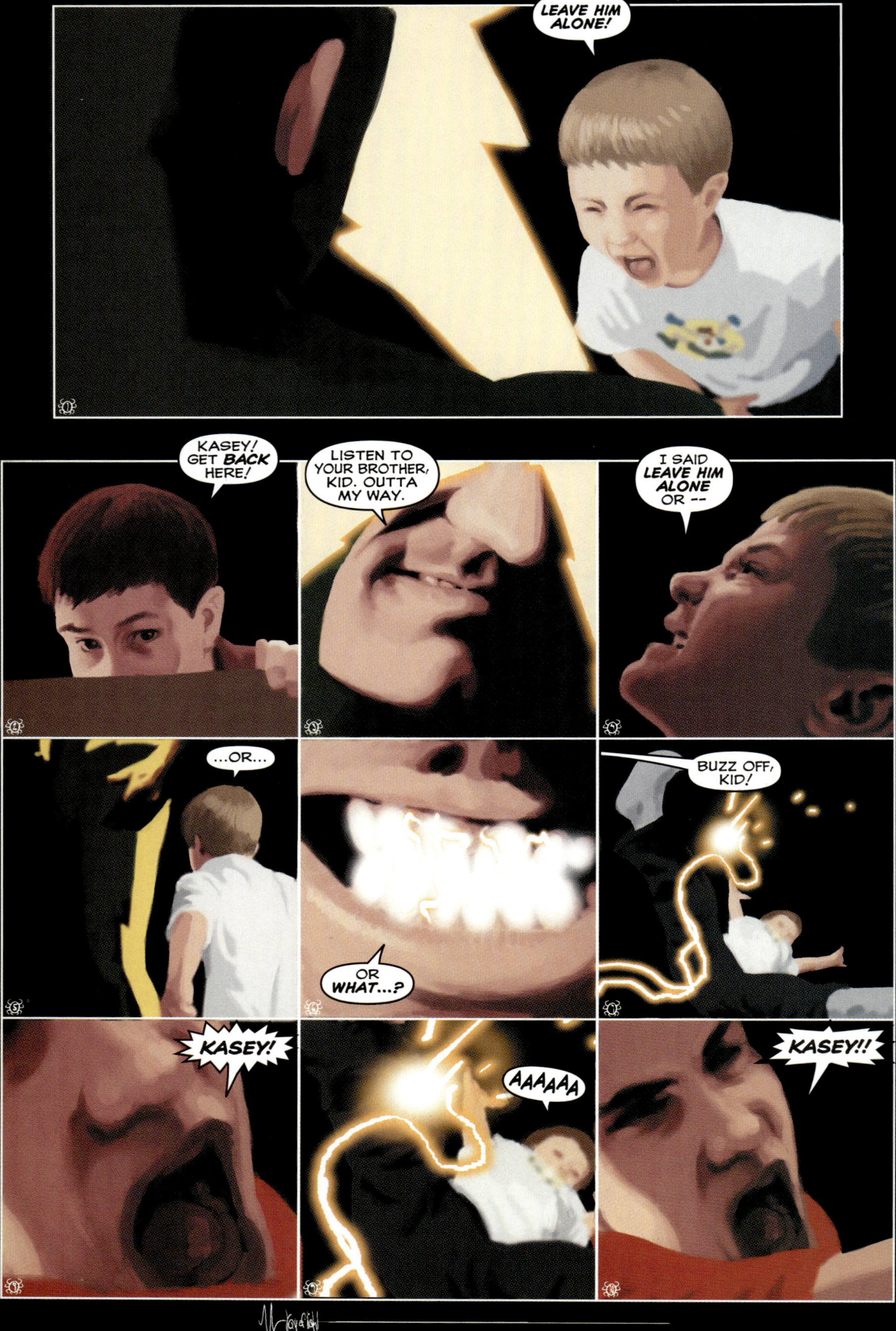

KASEY! GET **BACK** HERE!

LISTEN TO YOUR BROTHER, KID. OUTTA MY WAY.

I SAID **LEAVE HIM ALONE** OR --

...OR...

OR **WHAT...?**

BUZZ OFF, KID!

KASEY!

AAAAAA

KASEY!!

STAY AWAY FROM HIM!

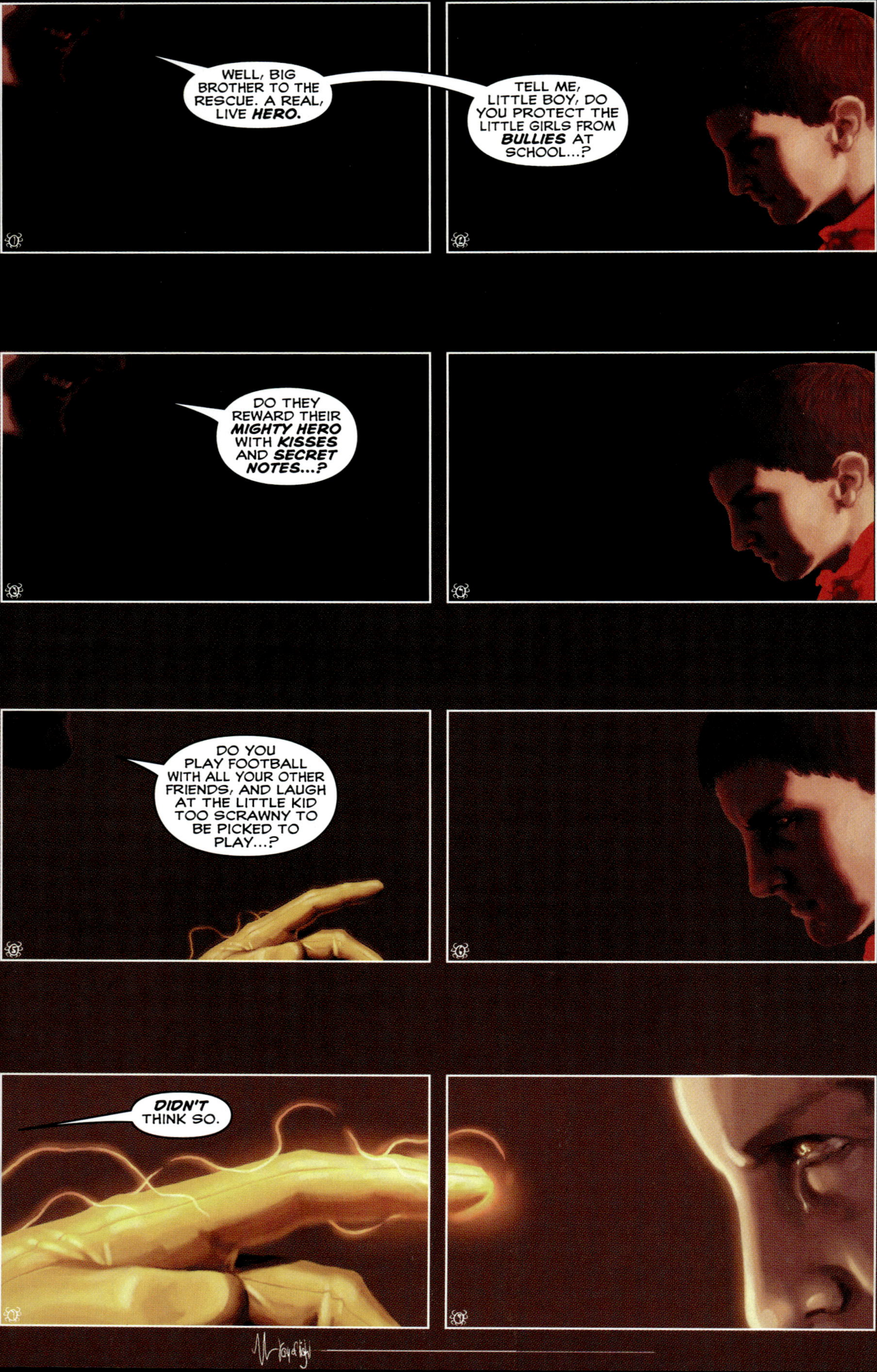

WELL, BIG BROTHER TO THE RESCUE. A REAL, LIVE **HERO.**

TELL ME, LITTLE BOY, DO YOU PROTECT THE LITTLE GIRLS FROM **BULLIES** AT SCHOOL...?

DO THEY REWARD THEIR **MIGHTY HERO** WITH **KISSES** AND **SECRET NOTES...?**

THWIP
AAAAAAAAAGH
WOW!

POW
SMASH
OOF
AGHK
CRASH

YAY!
YOU GUYS OKAY? WHERE ARE YOUR PARENTS?
OUR MOMMY'S IN HER BEDROOM.
AND YOUR FATHER?
WE DON'T HAVE A DADDY ANYMORE.
SORRY, GUYS...
...I CAN RELATE.
OH REALLY? A GUY LIKE YOU...?
TRUST ME.

AND I THINK YOU **DROPPED** THIS, BUDDY.

FIVE HUNDRED DOLLARS? YOU PUT A HOLE THROUGH OUR WALL...
...YOU ALMOST GET US KILLED...
...YOU DESTROY OUR ENTIRE HOME...
...AND FIVE HUNDRED DOLLARS IS SUPPOSED TO MAKE IT ALL OKAY!?
NO. IT'S NOT.
SORRY, KID. BUT THE GOOD GUY CAN'T ALWAYS SAVE THE WORLD. SOMETIMES HE JUST DOES WHAT HE CAN...
...EATS HIS BROCCOLI --

...AND *HOPES* EVERYTHING WORKS OUT.

I *LOVE* BROCCOLI...

YEAH...

YOU BET I AM.

I WISH WE ALL HAD A LITTLE BIT OF THE SUPER HERO IN US, INSECT-MAN.
CHIEF, I THINK YOU'LL FIND THAT UNDERNEATH THESE FUNNY PANTS AND HIGHLY FASHIONABLE HEADGEAR...
...IS JUST A GUY LIKE ANYBODY ELSE.

WITH SUPER INSECT STRENGTH AND GRAPPLING GLOVES?
DOESN'T HURT.
AND A COOL CAR AND UNLIMITED RESOURCES?
YOU FORGOT THE KICK-BUTT THEME SONG AND REALLY GREAT HAIR.
IF I WAS A PREACHER I'D BE WEARING A COLLAR, CHIEF. I JUST DO WHAT I CAN, EAT MY ASPARAGUS AND HOPE EVERYTHING WORKS OUT. NOW JUST REMEMBER...
...WHEREVER THERE'S A HANG-UP... WHEREVER THERE'S A BANG-UP...

...YOU'LL SPOT THE INSECT-MAN!!

YOU BOYS CLOSE THOSE WINDOWS... RIGHT NOW!... *COUGH* IT'S FREEZING IN HERE.

STAN LEE presents:

RAY of LIGHT

written & illustrated by
KAARE ANDREWS

COMICRAFT
letters

JOHN MIESEGAES
assistant editor

AXEL ALONSO
editor

JOE QUESADA
chief

BILL JEMAS
president

Raised by his beloved Aunt May and Uncle Ben, Peter Parker is a kind-hearted 15-year-old who tries to make it through every day of high school without getting picked on too badly. But Peter has a secret: At night, he sheds his studious trappings and dons the garb of the city's mysterious new protector — a hero for the 21st century ...

KRINKS SECURITY

FIRST UNION

YOU RENT-A-COPS THINK YOU MAKE ENOUGH AN HOUR TO TAKE ANOTHER HIT OF THAT?

THEN HAND OVER A COUPLE OF BAGS, AND MAKE IT SNAPPY.

I HAVE A FULL PLATE TODAY.

...BUT YOU WALKED RIGHT INTO THAT ONE.
WORKING STIFF
BRIAN MICHAEL BENDIS SCRIPT MARK BAGLEY PENCILS ART THIBERT INKS
JC COLORS RS & COMICRAFT'S WES ABBOTT LETTERS BRIAN SMITH ASSISTANT EDITOR
RALPH MACCHIO EDITOR JOE QUESADA EDITOR IN CHIEF BILL JEMAS PRESIDENT & INSPIRATION

WHO ARE YOU SUPPOSED TO BE? THE VIBRATOR?
MYB NOBE -- YOU PUFFER!
THWIP
THWIP
SPACK
YYYAAARRRGGHHHH!

MAN, I COULD'VE HANDLED THAT BETTER.
HE COULD HAVE REALLY HURT SOMEONE IN THE CROWD. I SHOULD HAVE DISARMED HIM BEFORE HE KNEW WHAT HIT HIM.
KRINKS SECURITY
HOW YOU GUYS DOING?
IF ANY OF YOU HAVE A CELL PHONE NOW WOULD BE THE TIME TO CALL THE --
JUST -- TAKE IT.
WHAT?
JUST TAKE WHAT YOU WANT!
TAKE IT.
WHAT?
THANKS...
KRINKS SECURITY
...BUT IT DOESN'T MATCH ANYTHING ELSE IN MY WARDROBE.
CALL THE COPS, WILL YA?
"DUDE, I COULD'A MADE A FORTUNE YESTERDAY."
"THEN WHY DIDN'T YOU?"

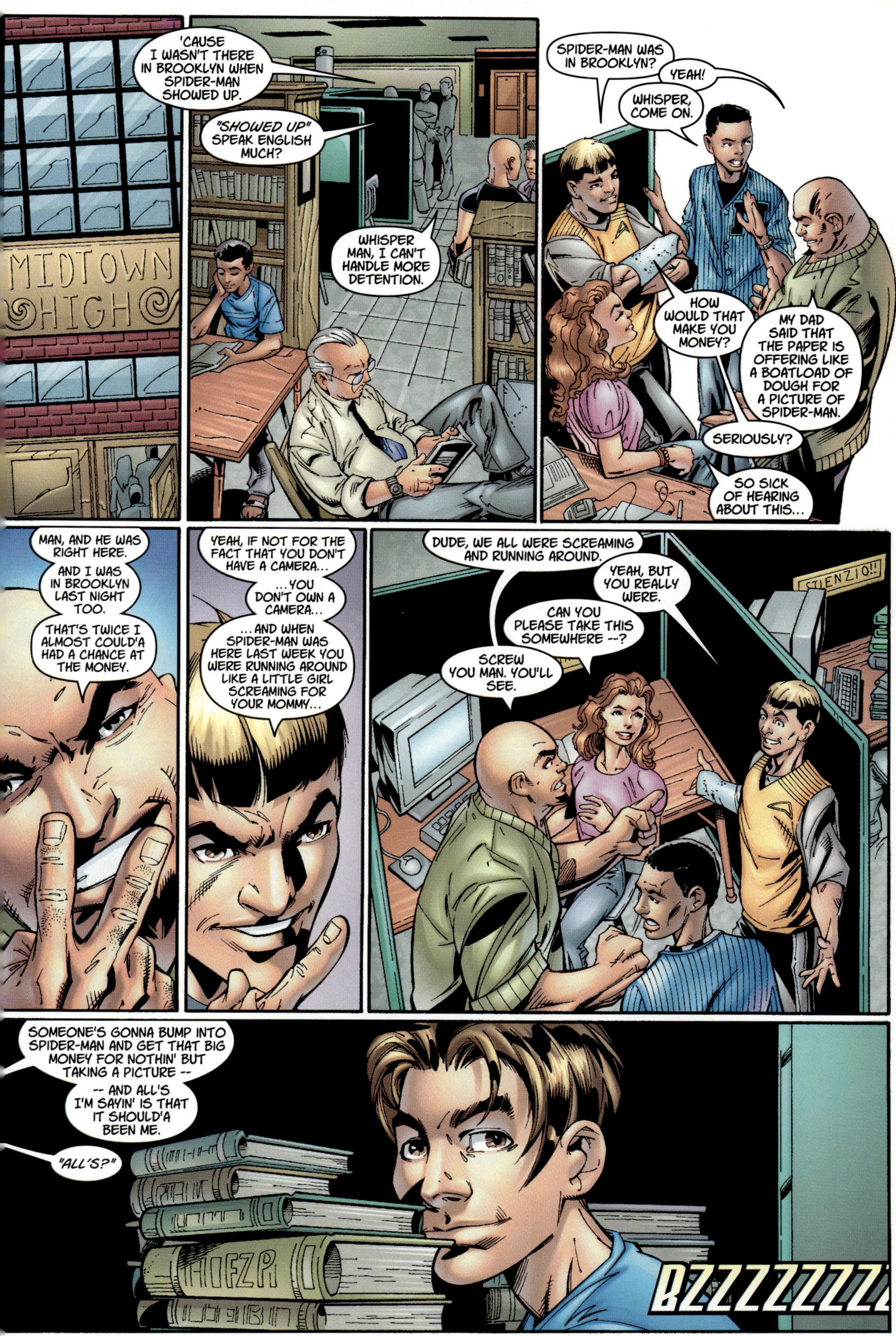
MIDTOWN HIGH
'CAUSE I WASN'T THERE IN BROOKLYN WHEN SPIDER-MAN SHOWED UP.
"SHOWED UP" SPEAK ENGLISH MUCH?
WHISPER MAN, I CAN'T HANDLE MORE DETENTION.
SPIDER-MAN WAS IN BROOKLYN?
YEAH!
WHISPER, COME ON.
HOW WOULD THAT MAKE YOU MONEY?
MY DAD SAID THAT THE PAPER IS OFFERING LIKE A BOATLOAD OF DOUGH FOR A PICTURE OF SPIDER-MAN.
SERIOUSLY?
SO SICK OF HEARING ABOUT THIS...
MAN, AND HE WAS RIGHT HERE.
AND I WAS IN BROOKLYN LAST NIGHT TOO.
THAT'S TWICE I ALMOST COULD'A HAD A CHANCE AT THE MONEY.
YEAH, IF NOT FOR THE FACT THAT YOU DON'T HAVE A CAMERA...
...YOU DON'T OWN A CAMERA...
...AND WHEN SPIDER-MAN WAS HERE LAST WEEK YOU WERE RUNNING AROUND LIKE A LITTLE GIRL SCREAMING FOR YOUR MOMMY...
DUDE, WE ALL WERE SCREAMING AND RUNNING AROUND.
YEAH, BUT YOU REALLY WERE.
CAN YOU PLEASE TAKE THIS SOMEWHERE --?
SCREW YOU MAN. YOU'LL SEE.
SILENZIO!!
SOMEONE'S GONNA BUMP INTO SPIDER-MAN AND GET THAT BIG MONEY FOR NOTHIN' BUT TAKING A PICTURE --
-- AND ALL'S I'M SAYIN' IS THAT IT SHOULD'A BEEN ME.
"ALL'S?"
BZZZZZZZZ

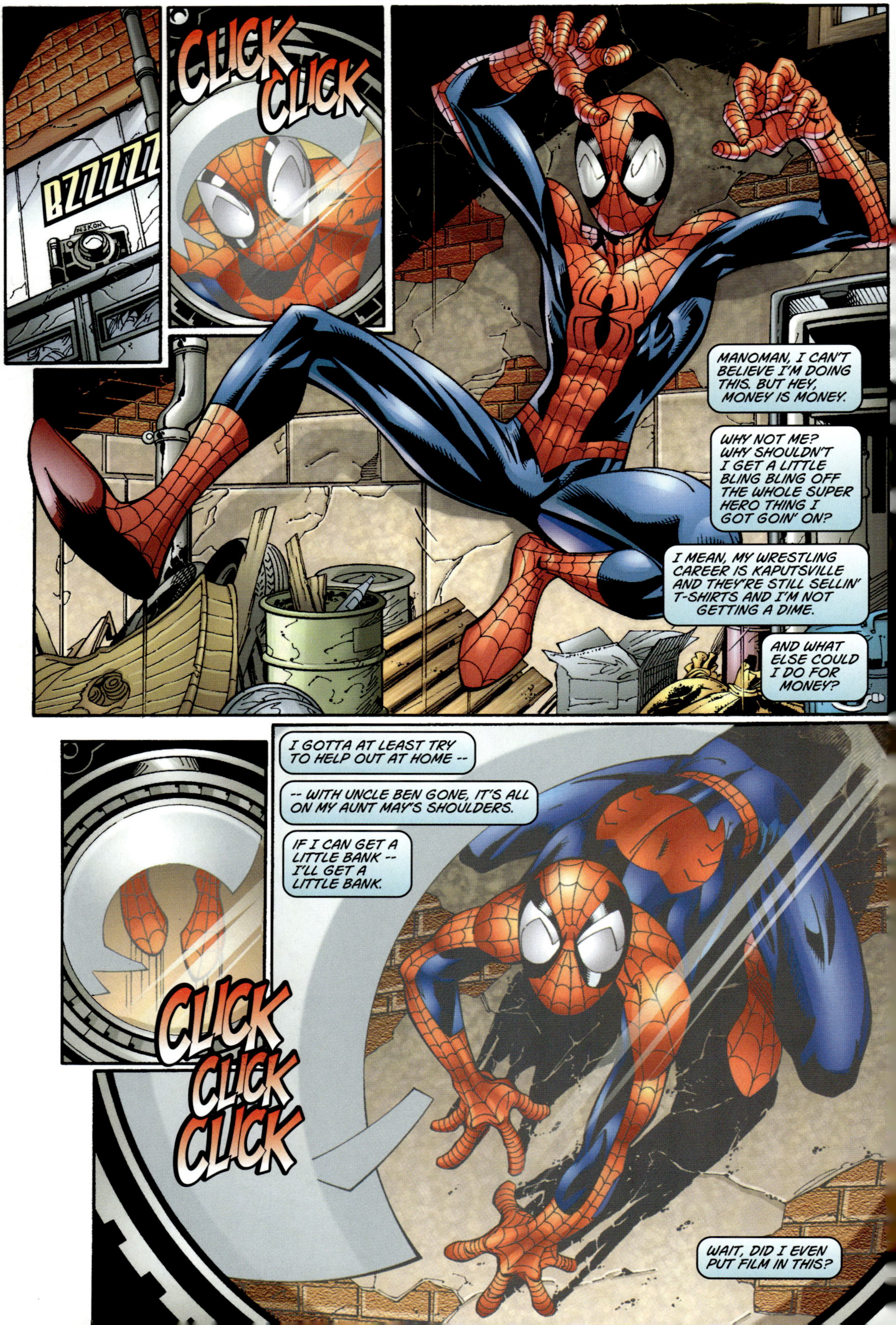

BZZZZZ
CLICK CLICK
MANOMAN, I CAN'T BELIEVE I'M DOING THIS. BUT HEY, MONEY IS MONEY.
WHY NOT ME? WHY SHOULDN'T I GET A LITTLE BLING BLING OFF THE WHOLE SUPER HERO THING I GOT GOIN' ON?
I MEAN, MY WRESTLING CAREER IS KAPUTSVILLE AND THEY'RE STILL SELLIN' T-SHIRTS AND I'M NOT GETTING A DIME.
AND WHAT ELSE COULD I DO FOR MONEY?
I GOTTA AT LEAST TRY TO HELP OUT AT HOME --
-- WITH UNCLE BEN GONE, IT'S ALL ON MY AUNT MAY'S SHOULDERS.
IF I CAN GET A LITTLE BANK -- I'LL GET A LITTLE BANK.
CLICK CLICK CLICK
WAIT, DID I EVEN PUT FILM IN THIS?

UH HI --
I --UH --
I -- I HAVE AN APPOINTMENT WITH A JOE ROBERTSON.
DAILY BUGLE
WHO SHALL I SAY...?
OH --
UH, PETER PARKER.

COPY!

THE CONVERSATION WAS OVER FIVE MINUTES AGO, ROBERTSON. ANSWER IS NO.
JONAH...
A CREATURE LIVING IN THE SEWER, ROBBIE? WHAT ARE WE? WEEKLY WORLD NEWS?
BEN SAYS --
EDITOR

"BEN SAYS."
BEN URICH? WHAT DID I TELL YOU? I SAID I WANT SPIDER-MAN. DID YOU THINK I WAS JOKING?

WELL, YOU GOTTA POINT THERE.
BUT I WANT SPIDER-MAN.
I'M TELLING YOU -- SPIDER-MAN IS OUR O.J.
JONAH, WE'RE ON SPIDER-MAN. EVERYONE IS ON SPIDER-MAN.
BUT WE HAVE NOTHING. NOTHING.

I MEAN, WHAT CAN WE DO IF...

EDITOR
FAR SCAPE

I'M WORKING ON IT.
"WORKING ON IT."

BEN, IF YOU PAID WHATEVER THIS PAPER COSTS EVERY MORNING TO SIT DOWN AND READ IT WITH THE MORNING CUP OF JOE, WOULD YOU BE INTERESTED IN A STORY ABOUT SOME CREATURE THAT LIVES IN THE SEWER?
YES.

WHO ON THIS GOD'S GREEN EARTH ARE YOU?
EDITOR
I -- I -- I -- CALLED.
I HAD PICTURES OF SPIDER-MAN AND --

WHERE'D YOU GET THESE?

HE CAME TO MY SCHOOL.

YOU GO TO MIDTOWN?

YES.

AND YOU TOOK THESE?

YES.

CRAP --
CRAP --
CRAP --
WHAT? DID YOU TAKE THESE WITH A DISPOSABLE CAMERA?
I...
CRAP --
CRAP.

YOU SWEAR THIS IS THE REAL DEAL?
OH YEAH -- OF COURSE.
YOU'LL SIGN A RELEASE THAT SAYS SO?
YEAH, I GUESS.
"YOU GUESS."
IT'S -- THEY'RE REAL. THAT'S -- YEAH.

JONAH -- THE KID'S A KID. CRAWL OUT OF HIS NOSE.
I CAN'T STAND IT!
HOW OLD ARE YOU?
SIXTEEN.
SIXTEEN?
WELL, SORT OF.
UH HUH. I'LL GIVE YOU FIFTY.
I THOUGHT IT --
GOD!

I DON'T CARE WHAT YOU THOUGHT.
YOU'RE A KID AND I DON'T KNOW YOU AND I'LL GIVE YOU FIFTY.
SOMEONE GET HIM A FORM.
I'M GOING TO LIGHT THIS PLACE ON FIRE!

WHAT NOW. MS. BRANT?
I CAN'T -- I'M NOT DOING THIS ANYMORE, JONAH.
YOU'LL DO WHAT I --
NO. NO. I'M THE ASSOCIATE BOOK EDITOR.
I'M NOT A FREAKIN' WEB DESIGNER. I CAN'T GET THIS FREAKIN' THING TO WORK!
IT FREEZES UP ON ME EVERY TIME I TAKE A DEEP BREATH AND I CAN'T I CAN'T -- I CAN'T -- FORGET IT. NOPE.

BUT WE PAID FOR YOU TO TAKE THAT CLASS.
IT WAS A ONE DAY CLASS, JONAH.
IF I TOOK A ONE DAY CLASS IN CHINESE -- I WOULDN'T KNOW CHINESE BY THE END OF THE DAY.
I DON'T --
ARRRGH!

HEY, WHAT HAPPENED TO OUR WEB SITE?! IT'S NOT COMING UP ON THE FREAKIN' BROWSER!
I DON'T KNOW! YOU SIT!
YOU CRASHED IT!
YOU SIT!

UH -- IT LOOKS LIKE THE SCRIPT'S IN A RECURSIVE LOOP.

A -- A RECURSIVE LOOP.
THE LINE YOU CHANGED IS CAUSING THE SCRIPT TO CALL ITSELF OVER AND OVER AGAIN WITHOUT A CONDITIONAL STATEMENT TO ALLOW THE SCRIPT TO EXIT OR STOP CALLING ITSELF.

NONE OF THE PAGES ON THE SITE ARE RENDERED BECAUSE THE RESULTS OF THE SCRIPT ARE NEEDED, BUT SINCE THE SCRIPT IS RECURSIVELY CALLING ITSELF, YOU'LL NEVER GET RESULTS AND THE PAGES WILL NEVER RENDER.

SEE? TECHNICALLY, WEB SITES DON'T CRASH. WEB SERVERS DO. AND THE WEB SERVER HASN'T CRASHED... YET.
IT WILL, IF OR WHEN THIS RECURSIVE LOOP MAXES OUT THE WEB SERVER'S CPU RESOURSES.
ALL YOU NEED TO DO IS ADD A CONDITIONAL STATEMENT LIKE THIS TO THE SCRIPT -- UPLOAD IT OVER THE OLDER SCRIPT.
I DON'T HAVE YOUR TELNET PASSWORD BUT JUST --
THERE!

HOW DO YOU KNOW THIS?
I DON'T KNOW. JUST -- Y'KNOW -- I KNOW IT.
HOW OLD ARE YOU?
SIXTEEN.
YOU GO TO LIKE A SCHOOL OR SOMETHING.
YES. I JUST TOLD --
YOU NEED A JOB?

SERIOUSLY?

YOU COME HERE AFTER SCHOOL AND WORK ON THIS FRAKAKTA WEB SITE FOR US.
BUT YOU GOTTA START RIGHT NOW BECAUSE I DON'T WANT TO HEAR ABOUT THIS THING EVER AGAIN.
HALLELUJAH!
I GOTTA -- UH -- I GOTTA CALL HOME AND ASK --
WHATEVER.

PARKER... PETER.
WHERE ARE YOU?
ARE YOU OKAY?

WHAT?

MY AUNT WANT'S TO TALK TO YOU.

THIS IS J. JONAH JAMESON.
UH HUH.
YES, I'M SURE HE'S A NICE B--
UH HUH.
UH HUH.
WELL THAT --
UH HUH.
UH HUH.
UH HUH.
YES I CERTAINLY SEE YOU -- UH HUH.
UH HUH.
YOU EVER DO THAT TO ME AGAIN AND I'LL TOSS YOU OUT A WINDOW.

WHAT WAS THAT?
I'M COMING. HOLD ON...
HELP'S ON THE WAY.
HELLO?

THOUGHT YOU SEEN THE LAST OF ME, HUH?

BLAM

PETER...
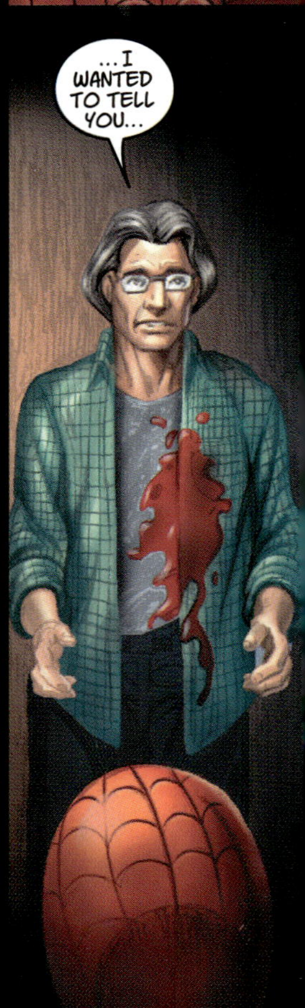
...I WANTED TO TELL YOU...

GGGAAAHHH!!
PETER!
UGHG!
UNCLE BEN!
PETER! IT -- IT WAS JUST A NIGHTMARE.

OH MY GOD! OH MAN!
JUST A NIGHTMARE.

WAS IT ABOUT HIM?

I COULDN'T STOP IT...

OH GOD!

How do Peter Parker's typically human wants and needs, hopes and dreams influence the actions and decisions of the larger-than-life super hero known to the world as Spider-Man? The web-slinger's chosen profession is a series of unrelenting tests, forcing him to ponder these and other life-altering questions on a daily basis! Can he rise above his fears and frailties to save a city in need? It's all in a day's work for ...

MOMMA, ROCHELLE'S HAVIN' A BIRFDAY PARTY!
BAM

SHE SAYS I C'N COME IF I BRING A PRESENT -- BUT IT'S GOTTA BE 'SPENSIVE!
S' GOTTA BE, LIKE, TWENTY BUCKS. THEY HAVIN' PIZZA FROM PIZZA SHED.

IT'S ON SATURDAY! C'N WE GO BUY A PRESENT FOR ROCHELLE?
MOMMA --?

GIN

MOMMA, I GOT HOME FROM SCHOOL.

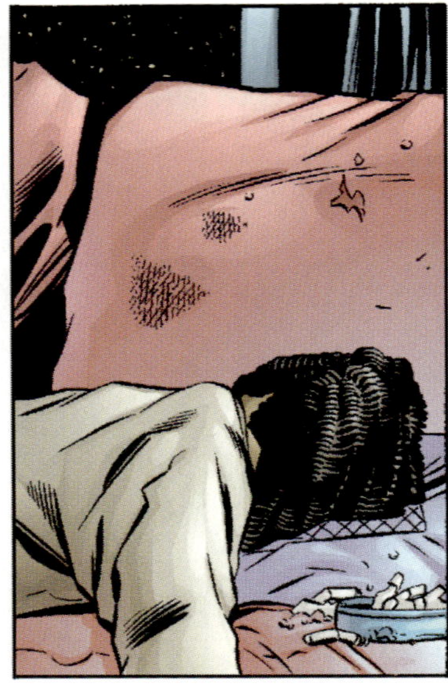

ROCHELLE'S HAVIN' A PARTY. SHE SAYS I C'N GO, BUT I GOTTA BRING A PRESENT --

OH... HEY, BABY. YOU HOME FROM SCHOOL ALREADY? WHA' TIME IS IT?

FOUR O'CLOCK. WHERE'S DINNER?

IN THE FRIDGE. DON'T BOTHER MOMMY NOW. SHE GOT A HEADACHE.

SO, C'N I GO, MOMMA? 'CAUSE SAMMY SAYS THEY DON'T EVER HAVE BIRFDAY CAKE --

-- JUST PIZZA...

BEER
BEE

SUPER-SETS #35
SPIDER-MAN

SUPER-SETS #
SPIDER-MAN
STATISTICS
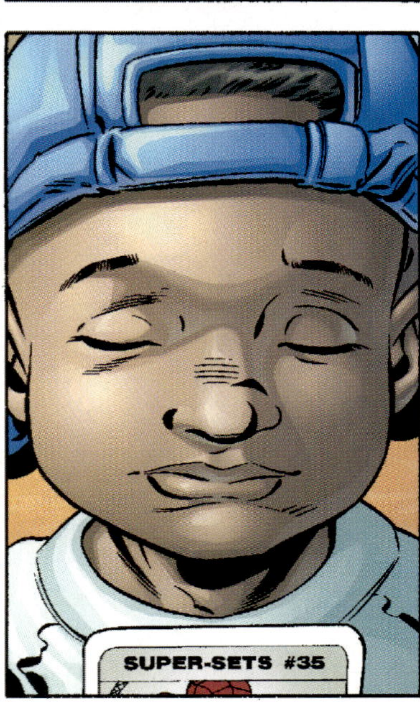
SUPER-SETS #35

HEROES DON'T CRY
HEYA, SECRET SIDEKICK!
PAUL JENKINS WRITER
MARK BUCKINGHAM PENCILS
WAYNE FAUCHER INKS
TRANSPARENCY DIGITAL COLORS
RS/COMICRAFT/WES LETTERS
JOHN MIESEGAES ASSISTANT EDITOR
AXEL ALONSO EDITOR
JOE QUESADA CHIEF
BILL JEMAS PRESIDENT

MY SPIDERY SENSES WERE JANGLY. THAT MUST MEAN YOU GOT SOME BIG NEWS --
ROCHELLE'S HAVIN' A PARTY! THEY HAVIN' PIZZA FROM PIZZA SHED!

PIZZA SHED, HUH? THAT'S PRETTY GOOD PIZZA -- I BEEN THERE MYSELF A COUPLA TIMES.
WHAT DID YOUR MOMMA SAY? SHE SAY YOU CAN GO?
KINDA. SHE WAS ASLEEP.

MM-HMM... I SEE. AND WHAT DID YOU DO IN SCHOOL TODAY, SPIDER-KID? LEARN ANYTHING INTERESTING?
FROGS AN' TADPOLES. MISS YEOUNG SAY' THEY BREED IN KOREA. D'YOU BEAT UP ANY SUPER-VILLAINS COMIN' OVER HERE?

OH, JUST A COUPLE. LET'S SEE... DOCTOR OCTOPUS AND THE SQUID, I SEEM TO RECALL.
I WHUPPED THEIR BUTTS REAL GOOD.

MY MOMMA FORGOT TO MAKE DINNER. I WAS SUPPOSED TO TELL IF SHE DID THAT AGAIN --

WELL, Y'KNOW, YOUR MOMMA LOVES YOU, LAFRONCE. BUT SHE FORGETS SOMETIMES.
YOU CAN ASK SAMMY TO SHARE AGAIN TOMORROW. HE NEVER LIKES HIS MOM'S SANDWICHES, ANYWAY --

A'IGHT. YOU RECKON MAYBE I COULD GO OUT ON PATROL WIF YOU TONIGHT --?
NOT SO FAST, SPIDER-KID. CAN YOU COUNT TO TWENTY FOR ME?

NOT YET --
WELL, THE DEAL IS YOU GOTTA LEARN TO COUNT BEFORE YOU CAN GO OUT ON PATROL. EVEN YOUR MOMMA SAID SO.
ONLY THE EDUCATED ARE FREE, LITTLE MAN.

NOW, I GOTTA GO ROUND ME UP A RHINO! SEEYA!

...SO, DID ANYONE FORGET TO BRING THEIR NOTE?
ANYONE?
ONLY THE EDUCATED ARE FREE
-EPICTACUS

THE HEROES OF CLASS 3B
My Dad
Fallon
Mrtin Luthr King
I have A dreem
ToNishA
Dr FrankN stein
JASON
Dudley Moore
HA HA
PAUL
SpiDR-MaN
LAFRONCE

NO? GOOD.
OKAY, DOES EVERYONE HAVE SCISSORS? I CAN HELP YOU WITH THE CORNERS, IF YOU LIKE. ROCHELLE? SAMUEL?
TREE
LEAF
KIWI
LAFRONCE

YO! LOOK WHAT I MADE!
OH, THAT IS SO COOL!
GLUE

"...ARTS AN' CRAFTS 'TIL LUNCHTIME..."
"...C'N WE DRAW YET...?"
"...ASK LAFRONCE FOR ONE OF HIS CRAYONS..."

SpiDR Man

MOMMY
ME
OnCE I Am at HoMM

MoMMY WATchs TVEY

SpiD R MaN is
CoMMing with ME

I DON'T KNOW WHETHER TO BE PLEASED OR ALARMED.

IT'S NOT THE SPIDER-MAN FIXATION -- THAT'S FAIRLY NORMAL FOR A BOY LIKE LAFRONCE. AS A MATTER OF FACT, I SPENT A *YEAR* TALKING TO AN INVISIBLE DOG NAMED SIMON WHEN I WAS HIS AGE.
IT'S ALL THE PLANES FLYING AROUND SHOOTING AT PEOPLE THAT I'M WORRIED ABOUT.
GO TIGER GO

MY NEPHEW LIKES DRAWING PLANES. HE'S *GOOD* AT THEM.
LOOK, I KNOW LAFRONCE IS A BIT *DIFFERENT*, BUT THAT'S *MY SISTER* COMING OUT. HE SAYS SHE'S BEEN HANGIN' 'ROUND THEM *GANGS* AGAIN --

I REALIZE HIS MOTHER'S BEEN IN AND OUT OF TROUBLE LATELY, ALEISHA, BUT THE LAW MAKES NO PROVISION FOR YOU TO FOSTER LAFRONCE UNLESS SHE'S WILLING TO GIVE HIM UP *VOLUNTARILY*.
YOUR NEPHEW'S A *RESILIENT* CHILD -- I KNOW HIS SITUATION'S NOT IDEAL, BUT IT HASN'T BECOME *DANGEROUS* YET. AT LEAST, NOT AS FAR AS DDS IS CONCERNED.

NOT *DANGEROUS?* LET ME ASK YOU A QUESTION: YOU HAVE ANY IDEA HOW *"NOT DANGEROUS"* THAT BOY'S HOME LIFE *IS* RIGHT NOW?
SAY WE GO THERE AND FIND HIM *DEAD* ONE NIGHT -- IS *THAT* DANGEROUS ENOUGH FOR YOU?

RAY, CALM DOWN --
RIGHT NOW, THAT BOY HAS THE SENSE TO RUN *AWAY* FROM THE GANGS, BUT HOW LONG YOU THINK BEFORE HE'S RUNNING *WITH* THEM? WHAT NEEDS TO *HAPPEN* BEFORE SOMEONE SEES *STRAIGHT* AROUND HERE?

I'LL TALK TO SOCIAL SERVICES AGAIN...

MOMMA! MOMMA!
BAM

THAT WAS MY STUFF YOU WASTED! MY STUFF!
WHAT'D I TELL YOU, YOU STUPID --

MOMMA... YOU OKAY...? WHAS' HAPPENIN'?

GO TO YOUR ROOM, LAFRONCE! Y'HEAR ME?!

DON' YOU TREAT MY SON LIKE THAT -- HE' JUS' A LITTLE BOY!
AAH! A-HUHH...

SNIFF...

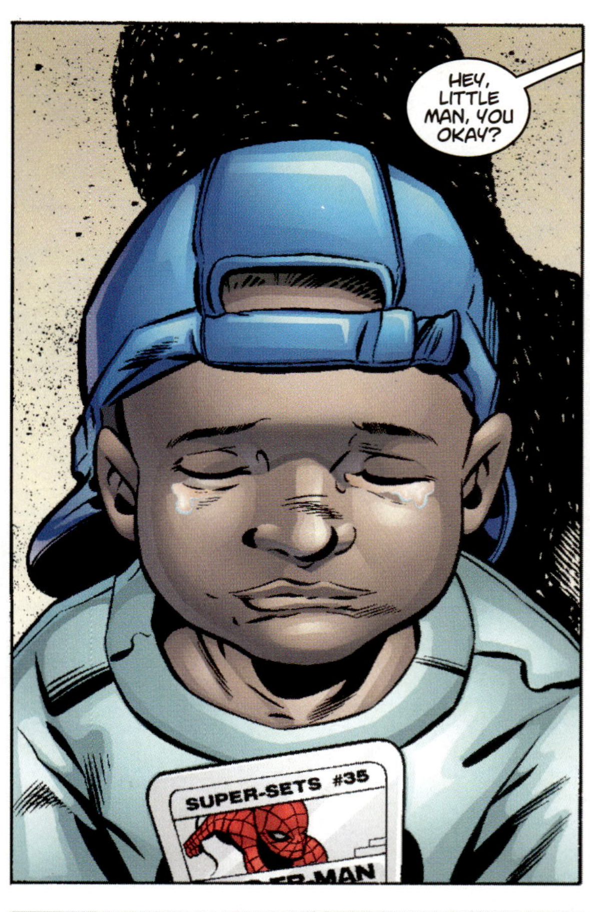
HEY, LITTLE MAN, YOU OKAY?
SUPER-SETS #35

HMM... MY SPIDERY SENSES ARE ALL JANGLY -- MUST BE TROUBLE IN THE AIR. YOU WOULDN'T HAPPEN TO KNOW WHAT *THAT'S* ABOUT, WOULD YOU?
DEVO CAME BY.

WHAT, *THAT* BIG POTATO HEAD?
SAY, I GOT A NEAT IDEA: YOU WANNA DO THE SPIDER-KID THING FOR A LITTLE WHILE TONIGHT?
Y-YEAH... OKAY... C'N I GO OUT ON *PATROL* WIF YOU?

SURE YOU CAN, SECRET SIDEKICK. WHAT SAY WE GO SMASH US A *HOBGOBLIN?*

...I DON'T UNDERSTAND... *SNIFF*... WHY NOT JUST FOR A LITTLE WHILE?

IT'S NOT JUST A MATTER OF WHAT YOU MAY WANT, MISS BENNETT -- IT'S A MATTER OF WHAT THE LAW WILL ALLOW. YOU AND RAY AREN'T MARRIED, BUT YOU LIVE TOGETHER -- THAT'S A PROBLEM.
LAFRONCE HAS TO STAY WITH HIS MOTHER -- HE'S BETTER OFF THERE.

BUT SHE'S SICK. IT'S NOT HER FAULT, BUT SHE JUST DON'T HAVE IT TOGETHER --
IS THAT SOCIAL SERVICES? LET ME TALK TO THEM.

HEY, I HEAR ALL THOSE RULES AND REGULATIONS YOU HIDE BEHIND, BUT YOU KNOW WHAT I THINK? I THINK YOU DON'T GIVE A DAMN. THAT BOY NEEDS AN EDUCATION AND A SAFE ENVIRONMENT, AND YOU DON'T WANT TO SEE IT.
WELL, HOW ABOUT WE SEE WHAT OUR GODDAM LAWYER HAS TO SAY WHEN I SET HIM ON YOUR LAZY BUTT --?

THE DSS HAS PROCEDURAL GUIDELINES FOR A REASON, MISTER WALKER. AND FRANKLY, I DON'T CARE FOR YOUR TONE.
WE'RE NOT EQUIPPED TO CARE ABOUT THE SPECIFICS OF LAFRONCE'S EDUCATION -- JUST WHETHER OR NOT HE HAS FOOD IN HIS BELLY AND A ROOF OVER HIS HEAD.
CO

CHICOPEE WOODS GOLF COURSE
LOOK, I UNDERSTAND YOUR CONCERN. BUT THE FACT IS WE'RE DOING EVERYTHING WE CAN --

AND THIS UGLY OLD BUZZARD HERE IS THE BLACK VULTURE, FOUND IN PARTS OF SOUTH AMERICA AND THE SOUTHERN USA. IT HAS VERY GOOD EYES AND A VERY KEEN SENSE OF SMELL.
CAN ANYONE TELL ME ABOUT VULTURES? ANYONE?
BIRDS of SOUTH AMERICA
BLUE-CROWNED MOTMOT
VULTURE
RHEA
BROWN PELICAN
HARPY EAGLE
FALCON

THERE HE IS, SPIDER-KID! LET'S POUND HIS UGLY FACE IN!
YEAH!

NOT SO FAST, YOU MEDDLESOME HERO!
WHACK
SPIDER-MAN!

GO TO YOUR ROOM, LAFRONCE!
...LAFRONCE? YOU HEAR ME, L.?

...AN' THEN, SPIDER-MAN JUMPS UP OVER THE TOP OF TH' BUILDING, AN' THE VULTURE GETS TWISTED ALL AROUN' AN' GOES "SPLATTOOIE" ALL OVER TH' SIDEWALK!
SPIDER-MAN C'N DO THAT -- HE CAN JUMP OVER FIFTY TIMES HIS OWN BODY!
THAT'S COOL, L.
COMMUNITY PARK

IT WAS REAL NEAT -- WE WENT OVER TH' EMPIRE STATE BUILDING. TH' VULTURE COME OUT FROM IN TH' SUN, AN' I SEEN HIM RIGHT UP NEXT TO US.
HIS FACE IS REAL UGLY. LEAS' IT WAS WHEN WE FINISH WIF IT!

HEY, LITTLE MAN! WHAT'D YOU DO IN SCHOOL TODAY -- LEARN ANYTHING INTERESTING?
VULTURE STOMPING, APPARENTLY.

WELL, THAT SOUNDS LIKE A GOOD DAY ON THE BRICKS.
C'MERE, SPIDER-KID!

I HEAR FROM YOUR TEACHERS YOU'VE BEEN DOING REAL WELL IN SCHOOL LATELY. YOUR PRINCIPAL SAYS YOU CAN DRAW LIKE NOBODY'S BUSINESS. THAT TRUE?

UH-HUH! WE DID A PROJEC' ABOUT HEROES AN' I DID SPIDER-MAN! MISS YEOUNG PUT MY ONE UP OUTSIDE SO'S EVERYONE C'N **SEE** IT!

THAT'S SO COOL, HONEY. AND DID YOU TELL YOUR UNCLE RAY THAT YOU GOT A GOLD STAR FOR EFFORT IN MATH?

A GOLD STAR, HMM? IMPRESSIVE.
AND HOW ABOUT YOUR MOM -- SHE DOIN' OKAY?
SHE FORGET MY LUNCH MONEY AGAIN.

WELL, YOU KNOW YOUR MOMMY LOVES YOU, LAFRONCE. BUT SHE **DOES** FORGET SOMETIMES WHEN SHE DOESN'T FEEL WELL.
HEY... WHAT SAY WE GO GET AN ICE CREAM? YOU LIKE CHOCOLATE?
YEAH!

OKAY... CAN YOU COUNT TO **TWENTY** FOR ME?

...SEVENTEEN, EIGHTEEN...
...SEVENTEEN...
...EIGHTEEN...
...NINETEEN, TWENNY!

WOW! IS YOUR TEACHER GONNA BE IMPRESSED WITH YOU, OR WHAT? I'LL BET YOU CAN COUNT HIGHER THAN ANYONE!
UH-HUH!

THIS SHIRT'S TH' BES', UNCLE RAY! I'M GONNA WEAR IT FIRS' TIME T' ROCHELLE'S HOUSE!
I CAN'T WAIT TO SHOW MOMMA --

OMIGOD, RAY...
...LOOK.

I SEE IT, BABY. YOU WAIT HERE, OKAY? I'LL GO CHECK IT OUT --

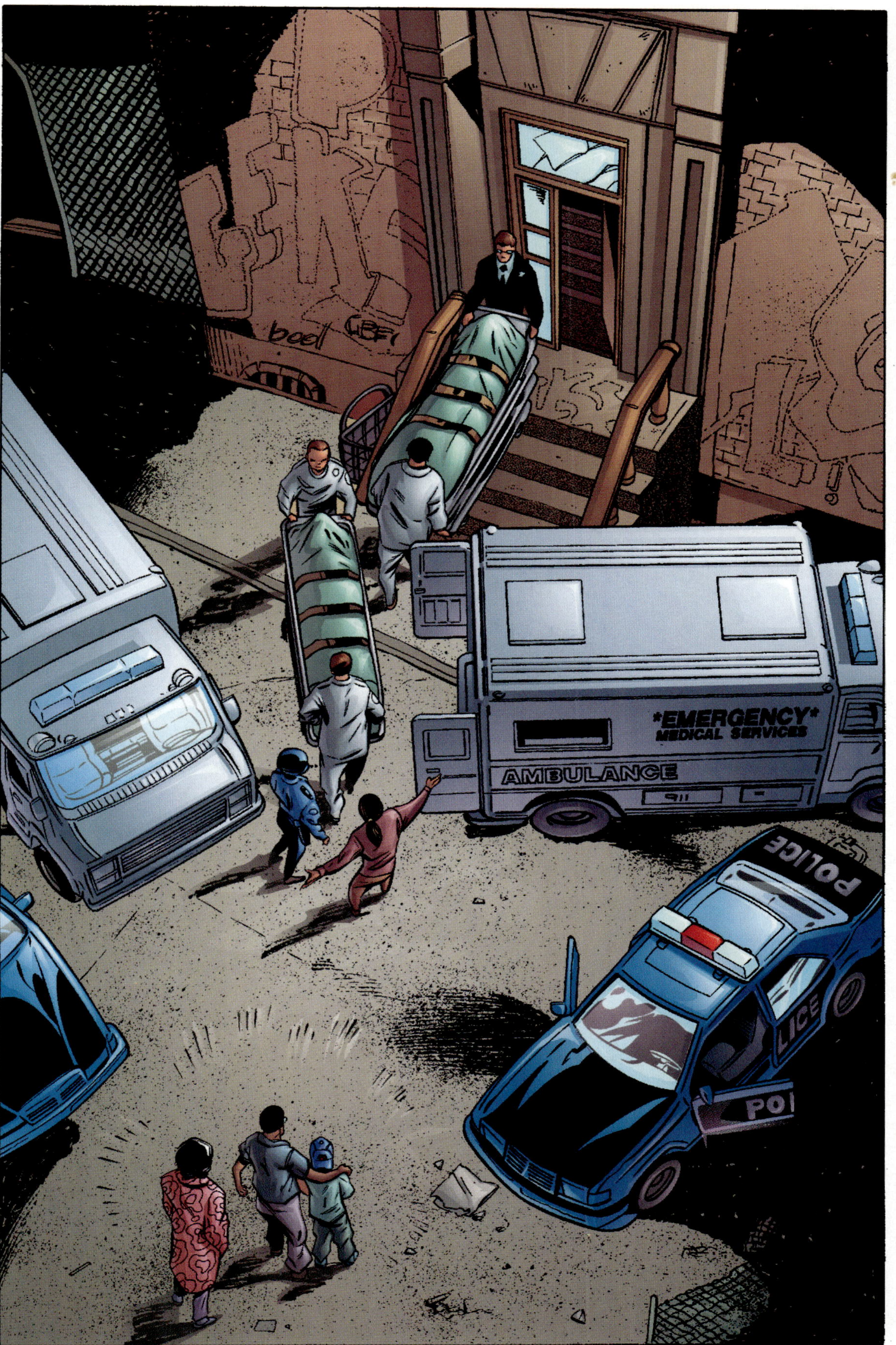
EMERGENCY
MEDICAL SERVICES
AMBULANCE
911
POLICE
LICE
PO

WHAT D'YOU MEAN, "SOLD IT ALL"?

I CAN'T BELIEVE YOU DID THAT. SOME OF THAT STUFF WAS LAFRONCE'S --
PFFT. YOU TRY TELLING THAT TO MY ATTORNEY. SHE OWES THREE MONTHS IN BACK RENT.

THREE MONTHS? YOU EXPECT TO CHARGE FOR THE TWO MONTHS SHE'S BEEN DEAD, YOU SON OF A --
HEY, HER LEASE DON'T RUN OUT TILL MAY. I AIN'T GOT NO NEW TENANT YET.

"HOW COULD YOU DO SOMETHING LIKE THAT? HE'S JUST A LITTLE BOY --"
"AIN'T MY FAULT, LADY. YOU'RE SO CONCERNED, WHY DON'T YOU FIND ME A NEW TENANT..."

ER-SETS #35
DERMAN

HEYA, SECRET SIDEKICK. WHERE YOU BEEN?

I BEEN AWAY. I GOTTA GO LIVE WIF MY AUNT ALEISHA NOW THAT MY MOMMA DIED.
I DON' KNOW IF I C'N BE SPIDER-KID NO MORE.

IT'S OKAY, LITTLE MAN. WE ALL GOTTA GO SOMEWHERE SOMETIMES. DID YOU LEARN HOW TO COUNT TO TWENTY FOR ME YET?
UH-HUH.

WELL, THAT'S GOOD. I NEED A GOOD COUNTER TO KEEP AN EYE ON THAT SIDE OF TOWN ANYWAY.
YOU WITH ME, SECRET SIDEKICK?

I LOVE YOU, SPIDER-MAN. I DON'T WANNA GO --
I KNOW, LAFRONCE. I KNOW.

BUT IT'S TIME FOR THE TWO OF US TO GO OUR OWN WAYS. TIME FOR YOU TO LOOK AFTER YOUR AUNT ALEISHA AND YOUR UNCLE RAY.
YOU DON'T NEED ME ANY MORE. FROM NOW ON, YOU'RE A BIG MAN, OKAY?
OKAY.
AND BIG MEN DON'T HUG EACH OTHER WHEN THEY PART WAYS.
THEY DON'T?

NOPE, THEY SHAKE HANDS.

SPIDER-MAN